WHEN NOTHING BEATS ANYMORE

Ineke Marsman-Polhuijs

Faithbuilders Publishing
49 Kingmere, South Terrace
Littlehampton, BN17 5LD, United Kingdom
www.faithbuilderspublishing.co.uk

ISBN: 978-1-913181-88-8

British Library Cataloguing in Publication Data. A catalogue record for this book is available from the British Library

Formatted by Faithbuilders Publishing
Cover by Faithbuilders Publishing
Printed in the United Kingdom

TABLE OF CONTENTS

Dedicated to Maria, who also lost her daughter, her fifth child. When she heard about Amanda, she reached out to me and shared her thoughts with me about being in the valley. She inspired me to write down my thoughts and what I had discovered along the way.

Acknowledgements

First I would like to share something about how this book began. In October 2018 I sent an email to Theo Veldhuis at Triple Boeken telling him I wanted to write a book and asking how it works if I let him publish it.

That same week, Mirjam van der Vegt phoned me, asking if I wanted to write a book. She wanted to publish a Bible study series and asks if I will write a volume for that. I am enthusiastic. That week, in my quiet time I am reading Daniel and think it is suitable and relevant for our time. She agrees and before I know it, I'm on a mammoth job, writing a Bible study book about Daniel. It turns out to be very good for my soul.

In March 2019 I hand it in and find that – partly thanks to this experience – I am ready to get started with the book that I actually wanted to write: a book about what helped me to continue to believe when it was dark. A book that I would have wanted to read myself when I was in the valley. I would just tell my story and what I discovered along the way, so that you, my reader, can take out of it what you can use for your own life.

Thank you Mirjam, for your conviction that this book needed to come into existence, for your comments, your thoughts, time and attention. It has helped me so much. This book would not have been here without you.

When this book was finally finished, I came back to Theo Veldhuis. Thank you, Theo, for your feedback in the last phase of this huge project. Your personal approach and your way of communicating has encouraged me so much. I really liked working with you.

So, this book had many previous versions, and each subsequent version became thinner, more compact, more condensed, more focused on who reads it. I kept what could be useful to many people and deleted what was only beneficial to me personally. That means that there is a lot that I don't tell and don't mention of what people around me said and did.

To my Love, my children, my parents and in-laws, my aunt, sisters and brothers, sisters-in-law and brothers-in-law, my friends, members of the church and all those mothers and fathers with deceased children who came to stand around me have done and said, was and is very important to me. Therefore thank you so much dear ones. Your prayers, words, presence, phone calls, messages, presents, meals, moments of attention have been incredibly important to me and to our family. Thanks for everything. I wouldn't be where I am today without every one of you.

Lisa, Yvonne, Marie-José, Janneke, Mariëtte, Marianne, Maaike, Lidia, Cor & Wicorel, Andy & Helen, Anne Lies and Marjolein: I want to name you personally. You know why.

Peter, without you I would not have managed to share my songs on YouTube. Thank you for thinking along, recording, playing along, finishing, refining and collaborating. What a process it was and what a great result! I hope we will continue to make a lot of music in the future.

Dear people of prayer in my WhatsApp prayer group: thank you for being Hur and Aaron to me. Your prayers, attention and encouragement are so important. I am very grateful that you helped me persevere and carry on when the process of writing this book was tough and that you kept reminding me of God who gave me strength and inspiration for this book as well as for my songs, blogs and other things that I may do.

Maria, Debora, Marie-Louise, Christine, Ruth and the moms at 'Lieve Engeltjes' (Dutch support group): you know the grief and the pain. You showed me that you can live with a hole in your heart. Your words gave me recognition, perspective and courage. Thank you for taking me into 'the group no one ever wants to be part of' and that you are there for me.

Steven & Marieke and Arjan & Irene: thank you for being so hospitable and giving me a place where I could write, think, cry and pray uninterrupted.

Christine, Tjitske and the team at Faithbuilders Publishing UK, thank you so much for helping me with the English version of this book. I am so grateful for all your comments and kind feedback!

Writing this book was also part of my journey through the valley. So I just want to end by giving thanks and with prayer:

Dear Father, thank You for giving me the strength to write this book. Thank you for the space given to me to do this. Thank you for the people surrounding me. Your will be done and Your name be glorified, honoured in our lives. Glorify your name in me and in the person reading this. In Jesus' name. Amen.

Mirjam van der Vegt

Foreword

Dear reader,

When Ineke asked me to write a recommendation for this book I immediately accepted.

This is a momentous book for you who are mourning – it introduces you to a fellow pilgrim who doesn't withdraw from tricky questions. I know out of experience how healing that can be on your often lonely journey of grief.

Grief is travelling to different destinations where you have never gone before. Experiencing different emotions requires tons of energy. Friends wonder when you come home again, but this experience doesn't come with an end date. If you ask someone how long they think this will last, they give ambiguous answers like: 'as long as you need'.

Were you in the city *Despondency* yesterday, today you wake up in the area *Expectation*. Just when you decide to stay a while, a bus comes to take you on an excursion to *No Man's Land*. It appears delightfully quiet, no one expects anything from you, but the bus already moves along for a long trip to the region *Exhaustion*. You try to hang in there with coffee. There is a passer-by who suggests spiritual songs as a remedy, but this pales so falsely into the barren landscape with valleys and hills, that you are relieved when the random stranger disappears again. Stillness is what is left, a welcome relief.

Suddenly a postbag is dropped from a helicopter, with all unanswered emails in it and also empty sheets of paper. You would like to write on them, but every sentence seems meaningless. So you stare at the pieces of paper – hours and days, and you feel so guilty of being so busy with doing nothing – although it feels like the most important thing you are capable of doing right now.

You'd like to make a travelogue, but where to start? And will it ever end?

With this book you're holding, Ineke wrote such a travelogue. Open, honest and raw, without losing the zest for life. She writes about the child she lost – but you can assuredly apply this story to yourself. What did you lose? What caused you great sadness? Was there a place you could go with your difficult questions? What did you find in the silence?

Mourning is different for everyone, so read this book with an open, curious mind. Maybe your experience of sadness is different than Ineke's, but her story shows how varied our feelings can be. Mourning is a way of love. To consider holy what has been, not putting it aside, but forming it into a worthy memorial site. It is okay to cry – it brings your soul to life and as Ineke shows: you don't need to drown in it. Her experiences form a path through No Man's Land. So that you know: I am not alone.

Liesbeth Koedoot
Foreword

A while ago Ineke shared her plans with me for writing this book. When messaging me she mentioned the title for her book: 'Als er niets meer klopt' (This is the Dutch title of this book. Literally it means: 'when nothing beats anymore', an expression meaning 'when nothing makes sense anymore'). Although this is a familiar line I often sing in one of our songs [Liesbeth is the lead singer of the Dutch worship band LEV], this sentence touched me deeply in relation to Ineke's story. *Als er niets meer klopt,* when nothing beats anymore, is what you experience as a parent of a deceased child, when the ultrasound shows the heart of your child not beating anymore. Sometime later, the publisher asked me to write a foreword. As the singer of LEV, I am much acquainted with the song that contains the same title as the Dutch title of this book. And as a mother who also lost a daughter, I am equally familiar with the pain of losing a child.

What a pure and honest book this is, about an immense loss and the raw, lonely mourning process that follows. Every chapter evoked recognition and understanding. How I missed that in the time I had to go through this. Ineke describes, woven into her story, her process with God in this time, a 'faithful mourning process' she calls it in her book. It is beautiful how she openly words her questions and doubts. Maybe that is what sometimes makes mourning even harder: when everything you considered truth, or obvious, also comes tumbling down, even challenging your rock-solid faith in God.

Losing a child is one of the worst things that can happen to a parent. Out of my own experience, but also because of my work as a psychologist, I know that this mourning process is very intense and difficult to understand for others. You can't process losing a child. You will always be the parent of your deceased and invisible child. That is how it feels for me too. My heart is broken, a piece is missing. I have learned to live with this loss, with this sadness. Over time the pain wears out a little, but you never really get rid of it. I wrote a song about it last year, about learning to dance in the rain. I've learned, and I am learning every day again, to seek my happiness in the Living One. Just as Ineke did, by trial and error. It brought me peace and wholeness: I can live happily with God despite and with my brokenness.

It's precious to read how openly Ineke describes her search, questions and doubts in this book. It moves me to read, through all her searching, questioning, doubts and sorrow, again and again her trust in Him, in Him who never lets go.

This book is about the heart; the heart of Ineke, the heart of God, my heart and probably also your heart. A heart that is broken, ripped apart, hurt. I hope that reading this book encourages you and that you will experience that there is One who stays the same always, even when you, because of what you go through, will never be the same again. I pray that you will taste and discover some of His never ceasing peace. 'Don't let go of hope, despite what comes, there will be salvation, for God is with us!'[1]

[1] This is another quote from the same song, 'God is met ons': https://www.youtube.com/watch?v=k0XC6r6Xieg

Introduction

'I thought I could describe a state; make a map of sorrow.
Sorrow, however, turns out to be not a state but a process. It
needs not a map but a history'

(C.S. Lewis)[1]

How do you hold onto faith when your world is falling apart? How do you stand firm on the Rock when the water is coming up to your neck? How can you experience God when all you feel is immense sorrow, or total panic? This is what I wondered ever since we discovered that our long-expected fifth child had died in my belly and I found out how far-reaching it is to lose a child. That you can be in deep mourning for months, without feeling anything else.

Before this happened, I already had been through a lot. In many difficult situations I held on to my faith in God by saying: 'Not my will, but Yours be done. I will serve You, no matter what happens (if I get healed or not, if my marriage becomes better or not…)' Later in my life, I added another decision. I wanted to be real. What you see is what you get. I wanted to live a life without secrets because Jesus says it will become public anyway. If not now, then later.

It turned out to be more difficult than I thought, because I want people to consider me kind, intelligent, musical, gifted, wise, sweet and caring. Sometimes I am, but often I am not. Hormones, sleeplessness, physical pain, irritations, fear of rejection, lack of self-esteem, or rather: trust in God; there are all kinds of things that make me pretend or puff myself up or diminish myself. Still I tried to be authentic, not covering up my mistakes and also not hiding better sides of me. 'For a righteous man may fall seven times and rise again'.[2] I learned to pray in another way and to allow the Holy Spirit to guide me. I trained myself to depend on Him, to put Jesus in the centre of my life and to become aware that I live in His presence.

When we found out that our fifth child passed away, I had already been trying to live like that for several years. But now I suddenly found myself between the pieces of all that I thought, believed and was convicted of. I recognize myself in the words of Kathy Beckers-Mansells, that losing a child for parents is like suffering a shipwreck. 'These parents are like drowning people, who see with some bewilderment that after a heavy storm their wrecked life is still there. After that, they look and search like beachcombers for the things that drift ashore to see what still has worth.'[3]

I searched for words to describe what I went through and named the blog I started some months later, *Broken but real* because I wanted to be real, honest and pure even then. I wanted to share honestly about how I mourned as a believer, as a mother, as a wife. Broken, yes, but also authentic, honest and vulnerable. I wouldn't have dared to dream that I would find strength precisely in doing that and, even though it's painful, I am marvelling at how I get to share my story with you.

Did you suffer a great loss? Do you wrestle with the question of why there is so much misery? Do you wonder how to keep having faith, or if you ever dare to trust God again? Then I hope and pray you will find thoughts in this book you can use in your journey and that you will be encouraged that God is still here, even when you do not feel or understand Him. Even when you don't trust Him anymore. While I wrote this, I prayed that you would see glimpses of His faithfulness and experience His nearness and His love for you. Even in the deepest pit and in the darkest valley He is Immanuel, God with us. He won't let you go.

In my book I tell you my story. To protect the privacy of the people around me, the names in this book are not their real names.

Living in the Present

Years after first postponing and then waiting, I am finally pregnant with our fifth child. I am thirty-eight years old and it is not a carefree pregnancy. I am happy that I finally conceived after such a long time of hoping and waiting, but I am also scared of what will come and what people will say.

I talk about it with Barbara. Every month we meet up to chat and to pray together. She asks me to be quiet. In the silence, a song I wrote some weeks earlier comes to mind. It is based on Psalm 100 and to my surprise I can now sing it with my heart: 'Your goodness never ends. Your love always stands. Your faithfulness until death is from generation to generation. Abundantly You brought grace'.[2] I notice that I am actually very happy that God entrusted me with this baby.

Still I am scared of what people will say. I am a bit older and I already have four children who each have special

---

[2] Originally the lyrics are: 'Uw goedheid eindigt nooit. Uw liefde houdt stand. Uw trouw tot in de dood is van geslacht tot geslacht.'

needs. Barbara asks: 'What is the gift you receive in this situation?' She has asked me this question before. What are the good things that God gives me in what I experience? What did I receive, for instance, from how people around me responded to the news of my pregnancy? I think of some friends who encouraged me and are happy for me. Barbara prays that I will become stronger. This pregnancy is desired and others might have their own opinions, but that shouldn't influence how I feel about this pregnancy.

After some weeks we decide to tell the children, though we don't know whether this pregnancy will go well. My Love, as I will call my husband in this book, says we usually allow the children to journey with us in all that happens and if we lose the baby, then at least they have experienced the joy of when things were going well. My belly is already growing, so I cannot hide it for very long. On Sunday, right after church, we ask the children to play in their rooms whilst we prepare the table. On each plate we put 'rusk with mice'[3] and then we call the children to come downstairs to have lunch.

Each child responds in their own unique way, one hugs me firmly, the other starts to cry that he has prayed so long for this, another keeps quiet until he is alone with me later and asks if he can help bathe the baby. I am deeply moved, bewondered and touched by what is sprouting up in my

---

[3] This is a tradition in the Netherlands. When a baby is born, all visitors who come to welcome the baby, will receive a rusk with 'mice': a sprinkle with aniseed, coloured pink for a girl, or blue for a boy.

children. They will become big brothers and sisters and they all realize that something big is going to happen and that they are part of it.

Because the children manage to not tell anyone at school, we allow them to call our family and share the news. For me it is too soon. I am insecure about whether this pregnancy will last and I have to calm myself down over and over again, to go back to rest, to God, to what I think myself. Whether this child will live or not, whether it is one or twins, whether they are supersmart or limited: he or she is here right now. This baby has been entrusted to me and I will take care of it. I will become a mother again. No, I *am* a mother again. I feel tired, miserable *and* very, very grateful.

A week later it looks like I am having a miscarriage. These symptoms keep coming back for weeks. One day it seems to have stopped and I am very relieved, the next day it seems I am going to lose my baby and I am shocked to the core. I feel it throughout my whole body. I keep telling myself that these symptoms might not mean anything. I had similar signs in all my pregnancies and it only once ended in a miscarriage. The other times it stopped after some days.

But now it keeps coming back. It is hard to attach myself to this baby. I swing back and forth between hope and acceptance one day and saying goodbye again the next day. In my quiet time I read Jeremiah 1:5 NIV: 'Before I formed you in the womb I knew you, before you were born I set you apart; I appointed you as a prophet to the nations.' Later that night my Love reminds me that this child is wanted and chosen and how it is worth every effort and that God already has a plan. I remember what I read that morning and I feel strengthened and confirmed about God's will for this child that seems to be still alive in my belly.

The next day I seem to miscarry again. I speak to myself: 'Still, my soul, be still and turn to God.' I don't know what is going to happen. One moment I am scared, the next moment I feel resigned. I am not carefree and full of joy. But over and over again I conclude: right now I am pregnant, right now this child is entrusted to me. So I try to take good care of my body and I pray, despite of the battles going on in my heart. God is in control. His timing is perfect. I lay my life and the lives of all my children in His hands. I choose to live in the present again.

Peace in Anxiety

When I am nine weeks pregnant we have an ultrasound and we see a beating heart in a mini human being of sixteen millimetres (5/8 inch). A miracle is happening inside of me and I am still, puzzled yet happy and grateful, 'Thank You Lord, for what You give to us. Bless it with Your smile, Your full attention, Your touch, Your word, in Jesus' name.'

Two days later it seems to go wrong again. It is so unexpected. I suspect the baby is fine, but it does shock me deeply. I want to pray, but I don't feel God and I wonder if He really speaks. I decide to just read His word once again. I want to hear His voice. Psalm 116 encourages me to think of all the times He was there for me. He is there for me now too. But still I feel unclear.

Some days later, whilst walking my child to school, I suddenly experience peace. I am anxious about a meeting I have to go to that afternoon, but I suddenly realize that I don't have to judge. I only need to have love and grace. This idea keeps coming back to my mind during the day.

Apparently God does speak to me. It is not in a dramatic way, but quiet and peaceful and I actually like that.

I have a feeling that, despite my unrest, I have to read the Bible. Aches and pains in my body keep distracting me, but I also feel determined and I pray: 'Lord make my will stronger. I want to know You. Please give me understanding when reading Your word.' I read Jeremiah 6:10 and I sense that it is possible to find joy in the word of the Lord. I long for that joy.

Because of my chronic hyperventilation I need to visit a speech therapist. She says that the most important thing I have to learn is to 'ground': 'You have to stand firm with both feet on the ground and have a good attitude. That communicates that you are really here.' I am perplexed. In all kinds of ways I hear that I don't need to do much, except to just 'be'. Well, there is not much more that I am capable of doing anyway right now. Find rest my soul!

A couple of days later, I take a long walk and try to listen to God. I enjoy the smells and the view and I suddenly remember what someone once said about me and my children. That they are my 'little flock' and that I can go before them, preparing the way for them. Jesus is doing that for me. Again, I become aware that I might not receive notes from heaven, but in what I read in the Bible and in what people say to me, I do 'hear' His voice and He is leading me. I can just follow Him and by doing that I already am an example for my children. I don't need to worry.

Surrender and Enjoyment

I barely have enough energy to give my kids what they need. It feels like I am falling short and I try to find rest in God, but it seems that everything has changed now. When I meet Barbara again, I become aware of how I long for His embrace and acceptance. I realize that I did not really search for God in all of this. As usual I ran away from my problems instead of praying and searching for answers together with God. I confess this to Him and then I pray for each of my children and for all that's going on. I also pray for the baby in my belly who is so present, but who I find it hard to give attention to. I pray for my Love, his work and his fatherhood and for me, my body and my motherhood.

When I am home, I read the devotional for that day in *Our Daily Bread*, a booklet that gets sent to me every three months. The devotional for today is about children. An adopted man writes: 'I have two mums who wanted me to have a chance. One gave life to me; the other invested her life in me.' And: 'When a desperate mother gives her child a chance, God can take it from there. He has a habit of doing that – in the most creative ways imaginable.' With gratefulness I realize that I can invest my life in my children and leave it to God at the same time. Both are needed. I surrender myself to God to do through me what the children need.

December 22. It is almost Christmas. Like Mary, I am pregnant. We have an ultrasound check and see our child move. After that we have lunch somewhere. We grasp a bit better that we will really have another baby. We talk about the sleeping arrangements and I remember what my mother, who has eight children, used to say: 'When every child has a place that is really his or hers and where it can be alone sometimes, it is good.' We decide to rearrange our children's bedrooms well ahead of time so that they can get used to their new place before the baby arrives.

I am reading *The Shack*. The main character, who loses his fifth child Missy through a gruesome crime, wrestles with 'The Great Sadness'. I feel the depth of his grief and how he wrestles with God. One of the characters says about Missy: 'She is and always will be your joy. That's enough purpose for her.' Suddenly I comprehend that I have my children to enjoy too. They, including the child growing inside of me, are a blessing. There is more to do than hard work: there is also enjoying. Living in the present. God will show me when I need to do something, but right now I need to rest, expect, pray and only do what He puts on my heart.

Do I Believe?

Still I am not able to rest assured. What is going to happen? Though feeling miserable every day, I don't want to be afraid and anxious for everything. In my daily Bible reading I am now reading Ezekiel. The prophet hears that his wife, the woman he loves, will die.[4] Ezekiel wasn't committing the sins of his people. He kept himself far from that and in that sense he didn't have anything to do with it. Still, by example, he had to experience such devastating loss. Why? God loves Ezekiel. He is a special prophet and an obedient man. Still, he has to go through this. I don't understand it at all.

I have been pregnant for almost fourteen weeks now. The symptoms of miscarriage finally stopped coming back, but I find it hard to focus on the baby. I wrestle with how meaningless life seems to be and struggle with all the things I have to do. The kids go to school, I work on a new song. Meanwhile a new person is growing inside of me who I may give life to live in this sinful world. Things have got worse with one of our other children. Professional help is needed and I feel like a failure. I feel guilty because we need help and because I am pregnant while the other children need a lot of attention. I worry a lot and I try to focus on God, but I don't succeed. Why do I sense His love when I am with Barbara and not here, at home? Why does *The Shack* touch me so deeply, but do I not manage to walk with God like that in daily life?

Sometimes I think I am just imagining what I believe. When that is the case, what meaning does my life have? I hold onto the conviction that I live because God wants me to, and to what I received from Him in the past. I used to be in a wheelchair, my hearing was worse when I was younger than it is now, and I used to be much more depressed. I received a lot of healing, though my body gives me problems now. It is as it is. I understand that I can come to God, just as I am, and with how I feel right now. I don't need to pump myself up. It is what it is: I am tired and I am pregnant, my body hurts and there is a lot going on.

The midwife phones me. I have permission to deliver at home because I do not have a medical indication anymore.[44] I am happy about that, but meanwhile I feel how I physically go backwards. I am often asthmatic and my body hurts. I have bad dreams and often I wake up in the night with the feeling that my child doesn't live anymore. I don't understand why I am so afraid of that. Happily, some days

---

[44] In Holland, delivering your baby at home is normal. You only go to the hospital if there is a medical need to do so, or if your home is not suitable, or if you really want to give birth in hospital. Because of the illness I had in my twenties, I had a medical indication to give birth in hospital.

later, I hear my baby's heartbeat when I have a check with the midwife again. I am so relieved.

Theo, a dear friend from our past sends me a WhatsApp message that he has cancer and there is probably nothing that can be done anymore. I can't believe it, but a few days later he texts that he has only six weeks to live. If Jesus doesn't do anything, he will die. In that same week we find out that our child we worry so much about suffers greater and more frequent bullying than we thought. I cry in silence, so that my child doesn't see it and ask for help from my sisters and friends via WhatsApp: 'pray for us'. One friend sends me an email saying that I first need to be angry. Forgiving the bullies can be done after that. First, allow those feelings to just be there. I am grateful she says that.

When I am on my bike the next day, suddenly a joyful song pops up in my head: 'Jesus is the joy of my life'. I am surprised when I realize that in one way or the other I do have faith for the future, also for this pregnancy and giving birth. Even if everything goes wrong, God is still with me and my children. It feels good to feel so strong in Christ.

But then I have restless nights and nightmares again. So much stress isn't good for the baby. I need to rest, but my heart and thoughts go wild. I try to sit down for a while and to just 'be', but I don't succeed at it.

In church the sermon is about grace and the worship leader tells us that we need to go back to the cross. That is where it all begins. I think of a story I read somewhere: a couple arrived at a prayer meeting. The man was drunk, but prayed out loud anyway, a muddled and incoherent prayer. After the prayers the host came to him and, pretending nothing happened, she offered him treats and asked kindly: 'Do you like cookies?' She didn't judge him, but made him feel at ease. Step by step God led him out of his misery. He and his family got saved and after some years he became one of the most loved elders the author had known.

That I have to think of this story now... I too want to be accepting and without judgment towards others, but maybe I need to be just that for myself as well. I find it hard to have faith and to trust God for the future. But through Jesus, through the cross, I am accepted. My children are accepted. I want to respond with acceptance and love towards them and others, myself included.

Little Girl

It is a girl! We have the twenty-week-ultrasound, the regular screening at the midwives' centre where the baby is thoroughly checked. Her heart is formed and her brains too. She has arms and legs and her skin is closed. The only 'but' is that she is one and a half weeks smaller than she should be. That is not good. We need to go to the hospital for a more specialized ultrasound.

We try not to worry. We celebrate the birthdays in our family that week, but my thoughts are with the little girl in my belly. With some people we share what is going on. One says that it will be all right, someone else says we need to speak growth in Jesus' name. I don't know what to do with what they say. I do believe that there is power in words and I speak life and growth over our little girl. I am so glad when I feel her kicking inside of me. But when I rest so that she can grow, I feel guilty towards the rest of my family. Still she is here and I feel her moving. She deserves as much care as my other children. I want to be there for her, but I don't manage to allow myself to feel the feelings that match that. Yet I know that being fully human means just that: a life with feelings and emotions.

My Love comes home. He attended a training course and shares what he learned with me: 'How could you expect a child to pay attention to geography when two minutes before class began, they were bullied in the corridor?' I think of the situation of our older child. I cannot expect my child to be friendly at home and to do homework when they have felt unsafe for hours and have been bullied. I also apply it to myself. I also can't expect myself to always be there for my children while I am so tired and scared of the future.

It's all alright as it is now. I write down what is bothering me and then I give it one by one to God. I cannot change the school climate and I cannot make my baby grow. I can do something about the atmosphere in our home and I can pray, take rest and pay attention to what I eat. I pray and cry until it is enough and I am able to be there for all my children. Not in my own strength, but in His strength.

When it is spring break, I go to Haarlem with my two youngest children. The guide in the Corrie ten Boom house says exactly what I need to hear: 'Thank God in all circumstances. He can work all together for good for those who love Him'. I think I believe it after all and I want to trust in it, even though everything seems too overwhelming right now.

At night I can't sleep. I share my thoughts with my Love and when I am still sobbing, he lays his hands on my belly and prays for us. Suddenly we both feel our little girl moving. We laugh relieved. At four I wake up and go downstairs to read my Bible and pray. I feel tired, but in some way I know very surely that He is with me and I conclude that it is stupid to only thank Him when everything is going well.

On Thursday February 23, 2017 we bike to the hospital for the specialized ultrasound. We find out that our little girl is two weeks behind in growth. It really is not good. I am in the beginning stages of preeclampsia: in the coming months my blood pressure will rise and my blood will become thicker and that can damage my blood vessels and organs. It can have consequences for my liver and also for the placenta. Our baby gets less nutrients and oxygen than normal. That is why she doesn't grow well.

In three weeks I have to come back and from then on every other week. As long as our girl keeps on growing, I can go home after the check. But if she stops growing, I have to stay there to be continually monitored. If necessary, birth will be induced. I feel defeated and scared.

Waiting

We bike home to an unknown future. At the pharmacy I hand over the prescription for aspirin they gave me – to make my blood thinner – and optimistically say I need it for sixteen weeks. In an email to family and friends we explain the situation and ask for prayer. I want our baby to grow and to blossom, I want to be healthy myself and I don't want to die. But nobody knows what will happen. This pregnancy can still end well. As long as she keeps growing, there is hope. All we can do is pray.

A friend mentions my little nephew, Brian. At the twenty-week-ultrasound my sister and brother-in-law found out that Brian had multiple heart defects. He would die at birth. We prayed a lot for him and every time I prayed for my sister and him, I felt hope. I did not know what it meant and I didn't dare to conclude something based on it, but I kept feeling hope whenever I prayed for him. In the summer of 2016, against all expectations, Brian was born alive. When I received the call with that news I cheered so loud that other people on the campsite came to ask me what happened. I was able to share the gigantic miracle God did.[5]

Now I pray for my own child as I did for Brian. But I don't feel hope now. Troubled, I read Psalm 139 again and again to convince myself that God saw her unformed body and that He sees her now as well, while He is knitting her in my womb. Very clearly I hear in my head: 'I am with you.' What does this mean? 'I am with you.' Why do I not feel hope, but only hear this? Of course I am pleased that He is with me, but I want to hear that all is going to be well with me and our girl. I want to feel hope. Just like I felt hope when I prayed for Brian.

I would really like to know what is going to happen. I sing the song I wrote last summer: 'God where are You? Do You see me?'[6] Suddenly it is terrifyingly topical. I feel pressure to be positive and to speak positively, as some believers say to me. But I know Christians who did die or who lost children. What category am I in? It seems Theo is going to die. Someone from our connect group died.

But I am not dead yet. What I have, has been discovered at an early stage and doctors will monitor me strictly. Only not yet. I have to wait for three weeks, because they can't act medically before I am twenty-four weeks pregnant. If she stops growing now, it will automatically end. I don't want to think about that. What if she slowly starves in my

---

[5] It is October 2022 now. Brian is still alive, though his life and his parents' life is far from easy. Brian went through a lot of surgeries. We still pray for him a lot and I still feel hope when I do that.
[6] Originally the lyrics are: 'God waar bent U? Ziet U mij?'

35

belly, in what should be the safest place for her? I am going to pay attention to every move she makes. It will be a good sign when I feel her kicks getting stronger. Again, I realize she lives *now*. However long she will live, she is my daughter. She exists. God wanted her. I tend to already withdraw, but if she would die, I want her to feel loved. I choose to attach myself to her anyway, however hard it is: you are my daughter. I accept you. I cherish you.

Another nightmare. I dream of people who want to kill me and my daughter. The fear of losing her keeps coming back but I have to accept that I just don't know. I don't know whether or not our baby will live outside of my belly. I don't know if my body can handle this pregnancy and if another pregnancy ever will be possible. All I can do is pray for protection, life and health, and to lay her and my life again and again in God's hand.

Because we probably won't be able to go away in the May holiday, we go on holiday now. I try not to worry about the baby, but I so desperately want to feel her and for her to stay alive. We don't know what will happen. Every kick counts. I try to rest because I want Susan to grow.

Susan. My Love and I both had this name on our hearts after praying for a name. Susan means lily and it is quite different from the names our other children have, who have names that refer to God. But this name keeps coming back and a dear friend sends me a message without knowing this: 'My prayer name for your baby is Lily, because that means 'little one' in my mother tongue and it is also just a beautiful flower.' What a confirmation! Susan, beautiful flower, today you are alive.

We try to give the children a carefree holiday, but I think they feel that mummy and daddy worry a lot. I pray and pray that I will feel our little girl and now and then I clearly feel her kicks. I call all of them to come and to lay their hand on my belly. It is hard to feel from the outside. I still feel no hope. My belly isn't growing really and I do not feel her moves becoming stronger. I do not have the conviction that all is going to be all right. What does this mean?

My Love keeps encouraging me to cherish her and speak lovingly to her and somehow this hard news helps me to pay attention to her more. Fear of her dying sometimes withholds me from totally loving her. But she is here now. She is alive and I feel her. This situation has positive effects too after all. I feel more connection with my Love and all of my children and I listen better to my body. I am better not to go on when I have pain or when I am tired. I take breaks more often.

Peace Before the Storm

After our holiday I go to Barbara. Again she asks what gift I received in this time and I share about how I live in the present more. I never managed to do that before. But *now* Susan is alive and I am intensely enjoying the moments that my children lay their hands on my belly and talk to the baby. Also I am finally able to let go more concerning the housekeeping. Our home is not very clean, there is more dust then there usually is, but I don't mind it anymore and that has never happened before.

I do feel that I am getting sicker and also there is a lot going on. Theo texts me that he is going to die and we hear the news that a dear family member has been admitted into a psychiatric ward. That night my Love and I go out, which is very rare. I enjoy being with him and being able to talk. We walk to the restaurant through withered leaves over wet tiles and search for words. Theo will die soon, our older child is having a very hard time, our family member suffers and our youngest girl does not thrive. We review all that is going on and suddenly we look wonderstruck into each other's eyes. We feel peace. We both have peace. Peace in our hearts amidst difficult and uncertain circumstances.

Sunday morning. Theo's wife texts that Theo passed away. God did not heal him but took him Home. I go upstairs, lock myself up in our bedroom, fall on my knees and cry until there are no tears left. I pour out my heart like water, as Jeremiah says so beautifully and don't hold myself in. After that I pray for everyone involved in Theo's life and for me and when I feel that it is enough, I get up and go to church. I don't hide my grief there, but it doesn't paralyze me either. This was good to do this way.

A day or two later I bike home after bringing my children to school. Suddenly I see very clearly how Theo is in heaven. The blue sky above me seems to open up and I get a glimpse of his happiness and future. Stunned, I realize that, though I would rather he was raised from the dead, he really is well and very happy. This is not make-believe. This is reality. I get off my bike and text his wife to tell her what I saw. When I start biking again, I have a feeling that this picture also has something to do with me.

I don't want to think about that.

The next day I feel an urge to prepare everything for the baby. We already have a room with a cradle in it. I am not even twenty-four weeks pregnant, but I want my baby to feel that she is welcome if she is born already. In a leaflet I read that a shop nearby sells baby clothes. I go there, but what they sell is all too big for her. Upset, I text the friend I planned to meet to say that I will come later. I take some time to process this. What is the matter with me? Why do

I cry? Reason and emotions run out of sync. Finally I drive to my friend and tell her what I am thinking. She is full of understanding and very sweet to me. She allows me to cry and prays for me, my five children, my family, the whole situation. While she prays, I feel something in my belly. Do I feel her move?

The next day I have piano lessons. When my teacher plays something beautiful to me, I suddenly feel Susan clear and strong moving inside of me. I jump up and I am incredibly happy and relieved. I so hope to feel her more often and stronger.

But that does not happen. I think I don't feel her anymore at all. In the afternoon, I phone the hospital and ask, worried, what I should do. How do I know if it is going in the wrong direction? The secretary consults the doctors but they can't do anything. I have to wait until Monday when I have the ultrasound.

It's Saturday. Theo's funeral. We see friends from the past. Some find out now that I am pregnant. They respond happily. 'Life and death', someone says, and I say: 'yes' while I feel something coming up in me that I firmly try to push away. When my Love and I walk in the procession to Theo's grave, we both have the feeling that we will do this again soon. I feel very nauseous. One Sunday and a Monday morning left.

In church I speak to someone who has had a premature baby three times. They all are growing up healthy. When I am home I receive a WhatsApp message from someone else: 'You have to speak life'. I go to my bedroom again. I feel so alone and left to myself. Should I just speak life really? I feel terrible, but it feels as if it is too late, pointless. Don't I have faith? If my child dies, would that be because I didn't speak life enough? I think of what I learned about healing and prayer: 'Ask God how to pray and what you should speak'. The only thing I keep 'hearing' when I pray is: 'I am with you'. I feel or think nothing else. So I bless my child in Jesus' name and meanwhile try to take care of my family.

I almost don't sleep anymore. I read about premature babies and incubators and it is not fun. I want a healthy, fully grown baby and I keep praying for that. Still I have a feeling that I need to be prepared. Besides that, I don't feel her moving anymore. Twenty-nine hours left until the ultrasound. I so hope our baby keeps growing and that I can keep her close after she is born, feed her and attach safely with her. That I can take her home to her siblings who are already crazy about her.

Still, I am not really present with full attention. I would rather watch movies all day so time goes faster and it is time for the ultrasound. But also now, at this moment it is important to be really present in the here and now. That is where God is. In the now, at the present.

I'M SORRY

It is Monday morning, six o clock. I didn't sleep well. My Love is already downstairs and when I tell him that I am very nervous, he says: 'Yeah, me too. I feel like I have to take a very important exam.' That is not a good sign. Usually he reassures me, but apparently I am not the only one who is full of tension.

Heavily burdened we bike to the hospital. Finally it is time. The three weeks of waiting, talking and praying are over. I am over twenty-four weeks pregnant, our daughter is viable, if necessary a doctor can act medically. There are meals in our freezer, I made a list of people who want to help take care of the children. If I have to stay in the hospital, it is possible.

'Mrs Marsman?' I nod and walk to the examination room and quickly lay down. With everything in me I hope we will see a bigger, vividly moving baby.

It is dead silent.

We see nothing but motionless silence and know immediately what that means. While the sonographer keeps looking for a heartbeat and doesn't say what we already know, countless thoughts pop up in my head, all at the same time. I scream soundlessly, cry, discuss, say short prayers until she says the terrible words no parent ever wants to hear: 'I am sorry... Your child passed away.'

Panic. Fear. Despair. Questions. All at the same time. How do I tell my children? Will my marriage survive? Where is she now? What should I do? I would like to teleport away somewhere in my mind, like I used to do when I was young and needed surgery again. My senses notice everything. Smells. Sounds. Feelings. Thoughts. Yet it seems I am not really there. It is too much. Too big. I want to scream from the top of my lungs and sneak away quietly.

After a short explanation we are brought to another room where we can be alone and wait for the gynaecologist. Totally different, we come out of that examination room. Do people in the waiting room see what's going on? That I carry death inside of me? Closer death could not come. When the door closes behind us, we firmly hug each other and then we sit down. I don't know what to say. He doesn't either. We seek words and carefully share what we think. God. Is she really dead? Dead. I feel I have to say it out loud in order to believe it. Our child is dead.

My belly doesn't feel that firm anymore and I suddenly realize it has been this way awhile. Still there is someone in there. Someone who passed away. How do we tell the children their sister died? What is this going to do to our marriage? I have read somewhere that a lot of marriages fail after the death of a child. Are we going to make it or will this be the death blow? We have been through so much already. Feverishly I search for a remedy. I remember what we learned in the time our marriage was very bad: to confide in each other what we personally feel and think, without expecting the other to reciprocate or even understand. Just express what you experience, think and feel.

I grasp the hands of my Love and hear myself solemnly say: 'I want to say to you out loud that I give you space to deal with this – I don't dare to say 'to mourn' yet – the way you need and that I take space to do this the way I need. I promise you to keep telling you what I think and feel. Will you do the same?' He nods and I ask if we can pray together. We intertwine our hands and cry at our Father who is in heaven about our child that has gone to heaven. We don't understand and we don't know what will happen now.

The gynaecologist comes in and tells us what the procedure is. When she is done we have to go to the social worker. I think it is a bit overdone, but I do want to know what is going to happen. 'You have to call the schools to tell them what happened', she says, and: 'At work, you have to call in sick for undetermined time.' I wonder if this is really necessary. We do feel a big weight pressing on us, but we also both have a feeling that we just have to 'take it in our stride'. We assume she knows better than us what is coming our way. She also explains that we have to tell the children in clear words what is going on. We should not soften it, because then the children might become scared of dying themselves. We should not say that their sister 'fell asleep', but clearly: 'your sister died'.

Even more heavily burdened we bike home. We do not really grasp yet that our lives have changed in just one second.

Death inside of Me

Our two eldest children are already home. By the way we walk towards our house they see something is very wrong. One of them looks full of hope at us and asks how Sister is doing. We cry and tell them she passed away. Expectancy becomes fright and then shock. We sit down with them, hold them tight, cry together. Then, one by one, our youngest children come home. They have never seen their dad cry and realize this must be very, very bad. We want to be there for them, but we barely realize what this means. Things need to be done: inform family and friends, arrange a funeral, make a birth and mourning card. I don't want to do that. But it must be done.

Our parents come to visit us. They want to be there for us and, because I would really like to have the cradle ready in case we can take our girl home, they finish the upholstery with the fortunately already washed lining. I want to comfort them, but I don't even know what to do with my own grief. Eventually I come up with the idea of having a small time of devotion the way we usually do with our eldest children. We drink tea and I read the Psalm I read every day these past months: 'Your eyes saw my unformed body; all the days ordained for me were written in your book before one of them came to be.'[5] God's eyes saw her unformed beginning. He knows her days, He has knitted her. This child, this dead child within me. We never saw her. But heavenly, divine eyes saw her.

We pray together and then the children go to bed. When our parents have left, we open a bottle of wine and try to comprehend, figure out and to find words for what just happened. I drink wine whilst I am pregnant. I never did that before and I feel guilty. But she will not suffer from it and I pant for an anaesthetic. My Love and I talk. Repeatedly I ask what he wants and try to articulate what I want. We are in uncharted territory. I don't know what he is like when he is full of grief and I also don't know myself in this state. We see undiscovered sides of each other and ourselves. I don't react the way I am used to. He doesn't react the way I am used to. This adds to all of it.

We make a group in WhatsApp to keep everyone posted. Around midnight I text:

'Everything is very unreal and intensely sad. As far as we know now, labour will be induced on Wednesday. It may take one or two days before the baby is born. Tomorrow we hope to prepare the funeral. When and how this will take place we don't know yet. Can you pray: that things concerning decision making and taking care of things will go smooth. That the delivery will go well, especially that the placenta will be born naturally and quickly and surgery won't be necessary (with premature births, surgery is often

47

necessary). That our children will receive enough support from us and the people around them. They begin to realize more and more what has happened and it is tough. Love!'

Again I hardly sleep. Death is within me. My child is dead. I keep repeating it because I don't believe it and still know that it is true. I cry, pray, write, try to think and hold my belly. Death has nestled itself in here, but I am still alive. It's not right that my body keeps functioning while I carry death within me. I can't come to terms with it.

I don't know how I will respond and I have feelings I never knew existed. I am afraid for what is going to happen, afraid that my Love and I will lose each other and that I will alienate myself from the people around me. So it is true: there are things you can only understand when you go through them yourself. I can't stand it. I want people to understand me and I want to be able to talk about it. If a friend had to go through something like this, I would want to know what it was like. So I decide to share exactly what I feel, think and experience in the WhatsApp group, so that maybe they will understand and, if I am honest, they will tell me that I am doing this right. I have no clue how to mourn and how to help children mourn. I want to do this well and I hope the people who read my messages will support me and us.

On the internet I search for books about dealing with the loss of your child and about how to help children mourn. I buy some with the money we saved to buy a dresser for the nursery. How do you give a good example of grieving? I feel a heavy load. I want to sink deep in this pool of grief and despair. But four sets of eyes are focused on me and I am very aware of that.

For these four children I am – with trial and error – an example of how to involve God in everything, how to see that He is the victor in every situation. But just now I don't understand my own feelings and I don't know what is going to happen. What I do know is that I want to protect my children from more misery than necessary. I couldn't protect them from death marching into our family. But maybe I can protect them from an inaccessible mother and uncontrolled grief.

Welcome Her

I want to pull out my hair. Drink gallons of wine. To be honest, I want to be dead myself. It cannot be that someone inside of me has died while I am still alive. At the same time, I want to live fully for the children who are still here. I barely sleep and I live in a daze. In the morning, James, pastor of our international church, comes to visit us. He cannot lead the memorial service because he is abroad next week and can't cancel his trip. Cody, one of the elders, is available to lead and though it is hard that our pastor will not be there, it is nice that Cody wants to preach, as he speaks Dutch and I want words in my and my children's own language. James prays with us and that is warming.

Next comes Emma, the undertaker. We don't know what to expect and we feel insecure. What is it like to deliver a dead baby? Fortunately, Emma knows what she's talking about. She gave birth to a deceased child herself. 'First, you need to welcome, because if you don't welcome her first, you can't say goodbye', she says. Suddenly we realize there is a journey we have to make before we go to a grave. It is good to talk with her. Though what she shares seems quite lugubrious, she is able to prepare us in clear words for what is going to happen. She tells us what our daughter's body might look like and how we can take care of her.

I am relieved and reassured. There is still something we can do for her: We can take care of her body. It still frightens me. I am a walking grave. I am not going to give life, but I do have to give birth. Emma says: 'You can't give her life, but you can still put her in the world.' Her words give me perspective and mother strength. To welcome. To put into the world. That sounds better than: give birth to a dead baby. Suffering pain for nothing. Preparing a funeral.

Despite how good and clear all these words are, I can't let go of the idea that I am a walking grave. The child inside of me doesn't live anymore and needs to be born. I am so not looking forward to that. I don't want this. I pray for strength, peace, everything I need to be able to welcome her. Saying goodbye will come soon enough after that.

In my diary I write:

'Tomorrow I have to give birth. Today we need to arrange everything we can. We have to bury our child. First I have to give birth, give her a name and then bury her. How immensely PAINFUL this is. Incredible. Everything was so perfect. The timing was perfect. She would be born on July 8. We could get to know her and get used to our new family life for a whole summer holiday and after that start normal life again. But July 8 we will not have a beautiful daughter. Tomorrow, March 22, she will be born at 24.5 weeks and after that put into the ground because her soul is with Jesus. Thank God I know that. Psalm 139 I have read again and again. I believe and I accept that God's eyes saw her unformed body. Tomorrow I have to deliver our girl into the world. Everything inside of me screams: NO NO NO! Let her live!'

In the middle of the night I get up again to write. Our daughter will be born today or tomorrow. I don't know what that will be like and have to live in the present now. I have swollen feet and thicker hands. Is my blood pressure rising already? I don't feel well, but that might have something to do with only two hours of sleep. I can't stop thinking. Our child is dead. I am going to give birth, but I will not come home with a living little baby that I can get to know, take care of and watch grow up.

I want to pray, to be close to God. But I don't succeed very well. When I am quiet, I start to cry. It is such a hard reality. Our child has passed away. The child we were hoping for so long did not make it. I feel guilty, angry and sad. I don't manage to really pray and quietly focus on God. Still I am not desperate. Just very heartbroken.

I Fear No Evil

It is Wednesday. This time we go to the hospital by car, without a car seat for the baby. We don't know yet if Amanda will come home with us and she will most likely be too small to fit in a car seat. Amanda. That is how we will name her. Susan Amanda. Susan, because we received that name after prayer. But now that she has passed away, it feels weird to call her by that name. So we choose to add a name that expresses how wanted and loved she is: Amanda (meaning: wanted).

When we arrive, we first have to talk with a lot of staff about the procedure, the use of painkillers and about what will happen with the body of our daughter. They take time to check if we are able to deal with it all. It is surreal to talk about all kinds of technical and factual stuff while I am intensely sad and impossibly frightened of what will happen. The nurse already wants to insert the needle for the intravenous drip. I absolutely refuse that. My youth is a long history of medical treatments that did not all go very well. As long as it is not really necessary, I don't want things inserted in my body. Especially not now, because it is uncertain how long the birth will last. A premature delivery does not have a predictable course. It can take a very short, but also a very long time.

The lamp above the door of our room is white. It means IUFD: Intrauterine Fetal Demise. Our status is clearly visible in the corridor: in this room there is a couple whose baby died in the belly. No one is allowed to go in there without permission. Everything, even bringing food, will be done as much as possible by the same nurse who only interrupts us if we are okay with that.

When the doctors, anaesthetist and nurses have finally finished their monologues, questions and insistences and I have received the first medicines to induce labour, we are alone at last. My Love and I with my pregnant belly and everything that will happen to us. We are in a cocoon. It feels sacred. A holy gathering with my Love and our Father who is in heaven and speaks to our heart. God is near. The peace we had last week is still there, although despair and unfathomable grief are there as well. My belly hurts. My inner being objects. God! Will this really happen? I don't want this! Amanda, my Amanda. Our daughter.

Someone texted me a link to a YouTube video yesterday. I listened, cautious, a little afraid that it might upset me. It was a perfectly fitting song. Now I play it to my Love, because every time the sadness overwhelms me, I listen to it and turn to what is true: 'We are not alone for God is with us.'[6] It is so perfectly performed: sad but clear, natural but rich, little words, but very powerful. The soloist sings high and sharp as my grief and pain, but not that high and sharp that it becomes unbearable to listen to. It fits well with how I feel and it tells me what I need to hear.

We are going to make a birth and mourning card. My Love draws a beautiful lily and I write a poem. We listen to songs to find out what we want to sing at the memorial service. Sometimes we laugh. Then we cry again.

I want to finish the card before I can surrender myself to what the medicine tries to cause in my body. The pain is intense. The uncertainty about how this will develop makes me feel panicky. Again and again I pray in silence. At one point suddenly something comes to mind: 'Even if I go through the valley of deep darkness, I fear no evil, because You are with me.'

It is the same message as when I prayed for our little girl: 'I am with you' and of the song: *We are not alone.* Apparently that should be enough, even now: God is with me. God is with me. I feel like Webster the scaredy spider.[7] But it does reassure me. In the year before I got pregnant, I studied Psalm 23 intensively and found out that God does so much more for us than we are aware of and that He is very close and involved. Though the pain is intense and the sadness way bigger than I thought possible, that rest, that knowledge, is a good safety net.

Welcome Amanda

We need a small basket to lay Amanda in when she is born. The basket the hospital has for us is way too big. I remember I have a basket in our attic. We phone home and ask if they want to search for it. As James wants to visit us, we ask him to bring it with him. We have made a card and have chosen some songs. Now the hour of truth is approaching. I need to surrender, to come into birthing mode. In comparison with my previous deliveries, it is a huge struggle. I feel resistance. I want to keep control. But to birth, you have to let go and allow your body to take over.

I haven't slept normally for almost a week now. I am very tired and also very frightened. The nurse suggests putting another bed next to mine so that my Love and I can lay down next to each other. We accept the offer with gratitude. I notice that the medication is beginning to affect my body, but it still can take hours before something really happens. We are tired and would love to huddle against each other and watch a movie. When we are settled, James and his wife Hope arrive. We talk and cry and laugh. Hope reads a Psalm to us. She says it is important to walk through the valley, to not run through it and also to not sit down. We just have to walk through it reposeful. I like that she calls it a valley of death. It does feel that way, but somehow I think I shouldn't whine. That this isn't that bad. That I just should just grin and bear it.

What Hope says corresponds to the text that came to mind earlier today: 'Even though I walk through the valley of the shadow of death, I fear no evil, for You are with me.'(Psalm 23:4 NASB) Except I do fear evil. I am very scared of what is going to happen. But I can't escape. Our dead child needs to be born. She cannot stay within me and she can also not stay with me. Just grin and bear it?

After praying for us, James and Hope go home. We are together again, back in our cocoon. We huddle against each other and watch Netflix for half an hour until I am not able to watch anymore. My body takes control. The pangs increase and become stronger. I get out of bed to catch the contractions. It's about time for the painkillers we agreed on. 'You don't need to suffer unnecessary pain' they said. But now there is another gynaecologist who resolutely says I cannot have the medication we agreed on. 'You'll become too dazed then', she says. 'You have to consciously go through this, that is important for your process. You can have an epidural, but we don't know when the anaesthetist will be available.'

I am in the flow now. It is not wise to disturb that with uncertainty about whether or not the anaesthetist will come. I decide to see what's going to happen and say that I will call if I want an epidural after all. I can handle this pain for another hour, but not an entire night. My Love texts my friends and sisters to pray for us and in our mailbox I find a card sent by people from church: 'Praying for the Father's arms to hold you close just as they do your little one.' I am very moved. These words correspond to what we wrote on the birth card: 'From mommy's belly straight into the arms of her heavenly Father.'

I am going for it now. The pangs come quicker and quicker. This feels the same as my previous deliveries, but suddenly I am very, very scared. I need to pray, not just in silence as I am doing all the time. I need to pray together and out loud. As a ritual, a marking. I ask my Love to pray with me and tell God that this task, the birth, is an impossible task. I look up and beg: 'God, I can't. But You in me. Oh, yes, I suddenly remember: not me, but You in me. You will give me the strength.' Suddenly I feel a conviction that I can do this. He will not let me be tempted beyond what I can bear. I surrender.

I am standing for some time while my hands seek support on the bed. Suddenly I feel she's coming. I carefully catch her and then lay her gently on the bed before me. I am almost euphoric. She is here! We have a daughter! And... she was born in the caul, so I don't need surgery! I am so immensely grateful. I want to see her. My Love runs away to find help and some minutes later we sit together on the bed while the nurse carefully opens the membrane. A tiny girl comes out. She has her little hand over her ear. She doesn't move.

O, little girl, come, I think. She fits on my hand. Our daughter Susan Amanda Marsman. So tiny and vulnerable. She doesn't live anymore, but you can see she has been alive. She has expression in her face. She is so thin. Did she suffer? What is it like to starve? I don't want to think about that, but now that I see her, my heart fills with love, emotion, compassion. O my little girl. I want to comfort you and hold you. But you can't receive it.

I place her carefully in the big hands of my Love. Now we see better how tiny she is. Way too tiny. But look! She has big feet, like her father. Her face looks like our other children. She clearly is our daughter. How can you be so proud and happy and broken with grief at the same time?

I want to call my mum, sisters and friends now. While she lays before me, I call them and tell how happy I am. I can't get my eyes off of her and I can't grasp that I have a daughter and feel so happy. I want everyone to come and see her. I want rusk with mice. I became a mother again, but our daughter lies motionless before me. The smallest clothes are too big; besides she is too fragile to be able to wear clothes. She is wrapped in a plastic mat. My child.

I thank God that He made her so beautiful and complete with nails and even some tiny hair. So beautiful. Not viable, really too small. But not a unformed body anymore. My Love writes in the WhatsApp group:

'Wednesday night, at 23:09, our daughter was born: Amanda. We welcomed her in this world, while she is already in the next. In this weird situation we first and foremost are brand new parents of Amanda and soooo astonished at how beautiful and delicate she is. Sadness will undoubtedly catch us up later, but right now we thank God for how the birth went and we are so happy with our daughter.'

What a remarkable cocktail of emotions. Joy. Sadness. Amazement. Despair. One moment we look at each other and see a new pappa and mamma. Though this is our fifth child already, we are overwhelmed with joy again. The next moment we see our own unbelief and despair flashing in the eyes of the other. Death is irreversible. Amanda is our child, but she passed away. We can't take care of her and everything in us wants to do just that. We became parents and want to take care of our child. But we can't, there is no need to.

Turn Your Eyes upon Jesus

It is time for me to take a shower and it becomes clear I need surgery after all. Inwardly I scream, full of fear: 'No!' I thought it wasn't necessary and I was so grateful for that. But now it must happen. I remember what it was like when I was a child. I am scared of the loneliness, the pain, the anaesthesia and the bossy, firm people around me.

The intravenous drip is placed successfully after three attempts. I am so glad I refused it earlier. As soon as the needle is in the right place, it hurts continuously. When they roll me away, I feel panic. My child! I can't leave my child behind! She needs to be fed. Who's taking care of her? Then it dawns on me: she doesn't need me. While the staff in their clogs efficiently roll me away, it sinks in that my child is deceased and doesn't need me. I feel a deep longing. The desire of a mother for her child.

I cry quietly but inwardly loud. I sink away in a pool of sorrow. Deeper and deeper. But I realize I need to be very strong now, to tell them what I need, so I won't go out in panic and awake later vomiting. The anaesthetist stands waiting for me. I ask for some time and attention to explain what is special about me. I hear myself say that I am traumatized and don't know how I will respond. I ask him if he can calmly tell me what he is going to do. I don't wear my hearing aid and my glasses. I am very vulnerable and only a body. But there is a soul in this body that needs clarity. Tell me what you are going to do. Do it serenely. Help me to accept what you will do to me because you have to.

Bad memories come to mind from the past when I was smashed like a doll from one bed into the other. I just gave birth to a dead baby and that was very shocking, and what I went through when I was a child was shocking too. It is all mingled now. I don't want surgery and I wonder why God is allowing this too. Suddenly the song we sang at Theo's funeral comes to my mind:

> Turn your eyes upon Jesus
> Look full in His wonderful face
> And the things of earth will grow strangely dim
> In the light of His glory and grace

It is a beautiful song, but how do you do that? How do you turn your eyes on someone you can't see? Quietly I ask God and then I suddenly remember what Jennifer Toledo wrote in a book I translated. You can use your imagination when you pray and God can use that to show you things. You can see with your spiritual eyes. In silence I pray: 'All right Lord, I turn my eyes upon Jesus. I don't know exactly how that works, but I imagine I see You and look upon You.'

I go under calmly.

When I wake up in the recovery room the pain of the drip stings as my broken heart. I ask the nurse to remove it immediately, but she is not allowed to do that. I feel alone and not known and I want to go back to my daughter. The nurse calls the ward and I try to rest. The minute I sigh I have to cry again. Amanda. To my surprise my Love comes walking in. Loved ones weren't allowed in the recovery room when I was young. It is so good to see him. But who is taking care of Amanda now? I have to go to her. Again, my heart shrivels. Nothing can happen. It is only her body laying there.

When we are back in the ward I want to look at her all the time, but I do sleep for some hours. When I am awake, I write in the WhatsApp group:

> 'Good morning everyone. We were able to sleep a bit. We both feel raw. Grief pops up and we are also tired. The surgery yesterday went well. Today the clinical geneticist will examine Amanda and we will have another appointment with the social worker. After that we probably can go home with Amanda. It is all very surreal. There are things we worry about, like how we are going to help the other children receiving Amanda. Please continue to pray for us and thank you for being involved.'

The clinical geneticist comes in and wants to take Amanda away to examine her. I feel nauseous again. What will you do with my daughter? Weird how the tiger in me awakes again. Just as it does when something happens to my living children. I want to be brave and stand next to my daughter.

I am allowed to go with her, but it doesn't help her emotionally, because she will not feel it. Unlike me, she is just a body. Because I don't need it myself to go with her, I let the geneticist take my daughter away and suppress the nauseousness. We eat breakfast and pack our bags. When she is back, we go home with our daughter. I am so glad that that is possible. I want to show her to everyone and feel like a normal new mother although I wonder how people will respond. Will my other children accept their sister and welcome her? Will my parents, parents in law, brothers and sisters be just as proud and happy with their granddaughter and niece as I am?

Of course I see she is deceased and tiny and vulnerable and that it must be hard to look at her. Rationally I can see and judge that she is too tiny and fragile to live in this world. But my mother's heart beams with pride. I think she is so beautiful, so ours, so really our daughter.

Mommy

We go home. My Love gets the car, and a nurse pushes me in a wheelchair through a backdoor outside. I have Amanda in her basket on my lap and I feel so proud that I want to show her to everyone and so sad that I want to hide myself. In the car we don't know what to say to each other. We drive home with a dead child. We have a child! The child is dead! Here a reversed exclamation mark should be applied. The contrast is absolute.

When we arrive home I go upstairs right away. I want to keep Amanda close to me as she is my newborn baby. But I cannot hold her close as she needs to be cooled, otherwise she decays. Emma comes in soon and assembles the cooling system. She places a kind of cooling element at the bottom of the basket that is attached to a device that keeps it cold. Then she lays Amanda down carefully in the basket and then the basket in the cradle wherein also my Love and our other children have slept when they were a baby.

Amanda is home.

I do take her with me now and then. When the youngest children come home for lunch, they have a glance and run away quickly. 'It is your sister!' I want to yell, but I so well understand them. It is their sister for sure, but she is not fully grown and doesn't make funny noises. She is quiet and tiny and she is too premature to show her to the world. She isn't an unformed body but she is not a full-grown baby either. Somewhat later the other children come to see her. They look death in the eye. We cry and hug each other. Inwardly I curse. We wanted to raise up another child in our family, but instead of helping children deal with a new family member, we have to help them mourn while we don't even know ourselves how to do that.

Linda, the maternity nurse, has come. She is a Christian and just finished a course about deceased babies. It wasn't her intention to come into a family with grief right away, but it happened to be so and for her it is tough too. She is very young, but it is nice to have someone in our home who is not intensely sad and who can help making sure that our children who are alive are doing well. Someone who also believes there is life after death and also prays when she needs wisdom. We are six people with each their own grief. We want to support each other but it is hard to focus on someone else when you're overwhelmed by emotions. I hope this young woman can support the children where I can't right now.

Then the photographer of *Make a Memory* comes in. A complete stranger, but a respectful and friendly man looks thoughtfully at Amanda. He names what he sees and how Amanda has everything and takes pictures of her hands, feet and other details. He tells what he sees so that, together with our children, we can admire her. It visibly helps them to accept and welcome her. I feel deep gratitude towards this artist. He uses his talent to help us mourn. It also puts new grief in the spotlight: we don't know what she would look like if she was a full-grown baby, and never will.

At night I do what I do every night before I go to sleep. I pass by all my children to whisper that I love them and to bless them in Jesus' name. I also pass by Amanda. Then it hits me severely: I have five children now, but my youngest doesn't need my words. I want to be with her, nurse her and get to know her, but she does not need *me*. I feel as if I choke. I am a postnatal woman who goes through everything a new mom goes through, without the joy of watching a satisfied, sleeping baby.

The next day there is a package on our doorstep. In it there is a treat and a small box with a postcard. In the box I find a small golden necklace with a heart. It looks costly. On the card there are words a woman from church has written down on behalf of Amanda:

If I could be the voice of the little one
Let me just say:
Thank you for carrying me under your heart
It was indeed a joyful time
Growing and stretching in your beautiful *buik*

The time given to us was way too short

---

[7] 'Buik' is the Dutch word for 'belly'.

Don't understand this mystery at all
I came and I went
Straight to the Lord.
From your *buik* to the heavens share
And when your time will also come
I'll be waiting here for you mom
I really hope that this pain won't last long
And that your heart would be fully restored
filled to the brim with new hopes and my love
If I could speak, I want you to know
you are my mom with the heart of Gold

I read, reread and read again. Tears keep coming. *Mom.* I am her mom. I am mom. I read what I apparently, according to my deep sobs, want to hear the most. I took care of her well. She had a good time while she was with me. She is happy that I am her mother. It is okay. Though it really isn't.

69

Maternity Visit

My sisters and friends come. I want to show my little girl and share our bitter happiness with them. It is so good to see that they too marvel about Amanda and make the effort to see us not only as mourning people, but also meet us as a father and mother. Brand new parents of a dead baby, but still a baby. Not everyone wants to see Amanda. That hurts, though I understand.

Again and again I go and sit next to her cradle, watch her and see the beauty. The mighty hand of the Creator. So perfectly made, known by Him from her beginning. She is beautiful, Lord, Your works are perfect. She is Yours and You have entrusted her to us, for far too short a time I think. She should have lived longer, to live past me. I want to see her searching mouth, hear her cry, feel her grasping hands, her first laugh, her sounds. I want to look in her eyes and show her she is wanted, loved, cherished and protected. But her eyes did not see the light of day, her lungs didn't get oxygen, we didn't hear her voice. Her hand didn't squeeze my finger, her mouth did not search my breast.

Carefully I take her in my hands. She lays there still, with her little eyes open. She looks content without looking. She is delicate and totally complete. Nails, toes, fingers, ribs, elbows, knees, bottom, ears, nose, mouth, even some hair on her head. I say what David said: 'Lord, how marvellous are your works, my soul knows that very well.'(Psalm 139:14 NKJV) I am so grateful that God made the effort to make her so beautiful. I lift my hands with her in them up and say again out loud: 'I entrust her to You Lord, she was Yours, she is Yours and she will be Yours. It hurts so much. Please come into this pain, Lord.'

That it hurts so much. That you can have so much pain. That your heart is torn apart and nothing appears to be the same anymore. I don't know what to do and search for words for what I feel. Sometimes I find some. In the WhatsApp group I try to tell how it feels precisely. But most of the time it is too dark to say it. I don't dare to tell it. I don't want to drag others with me in my misery and perhaps I am also ashamed that it is so dark inside of me.

That night I am sitting at the table with a glass of wine and my diary and realize again that I need to feel the pain and the grief and also to go to God with all of this. I remember what I read somewhere: 'Every loss can be filled with God', or something like that. God can fill the hole in my heart and I want to allow that. But then I need to acknowledge the loss. I lost my child. It hurts so much that I can't really allow it.

Even my body yearns for Amanda. I want to nurse her, sing to her, cherish her and watch her grow. I want to keep her with me until she is big enough to take her own place. And

I want to see her sisters playing with her and her brothers taking care of her and that they, when they are grown up, will be friends for life. But I held her again and I am very aware that the time will soon come that we have to bring her to her grave. She is not here. She lives with Christ until He comes back. Then we will meet again. While I think about this, someone texts me: 'Listen quietly to this song'. Bizarre. The song is the same song I sent to Theo's widow last week. 'Still, my soul be still.'

In the morning of Friday March 24 my Love writes in the WhatsApp group:

> 'Slowly grief begins to get through. Amanda really doesn't breathe. She really doesn't move her little fingers. She is dead silent. Today, together with the children I am going to choose a place for her grave at the graveyard where we will lay her down coming Monday.'

They choose a nice place for Amanda. I am glad my Love didn't have to do this alone. I feel weak and mournful and I am thirsty all the time. Linda says it's because of all the crying.

So this is grief. My dancing turned into mourning. The valley of deep darkness. I have to give my loss to God so He can come in it. But I want my daughter. She is mine. She belongs with me. Yet when I hold her it is so pointless. She does not respond. The pit I sink in turns out to be deeper than I thought. Lord, help. Everything inside me howls her name. When I look at my Love I see she has his lips. I see my older daughter and realize Amanda will never be so beautiful and big here on earth. God! Please come. Help me, rescue me.

She is deteriorating. On Saturday I rather don't want everyone to see her anymore. It is clear we cannot keep her here. We have to bury her and that moment is getting closer. We live very intensely. We want to be there for the children and to hide our grief from them, while we also want to be with Amanda as much as possible.

Happily there are people helping us. My sister came to give her attention to the children. Friends from church took the children for a walk yesterday. This afternoon my brother and his family will come and take the children to the beach. Tomorrow morning Linda will go outside with them. My Love and I keep trying to find each other, but it is hard to tell everything and to listen to each other. He is full of grief as well. I do appreciate that he shares what he feels and to realize that he loves her just as much as I do and finds it just as awful.

It is Sunday afternoon when I find out that I didn't give him enough space. For him it is also the last day with his youngest daughter. But I was sitting next to her cradle with a friend. Fortunately he eventually comes in to tell me that he wants the visitors to leave so that he can have time with Amanda, with and without me. Ashamed I embrace him and give him the space he needs and deserves. This daddy with his dead child.

I feel guilty but at the same time I know I could not do it differently. Grief apparently makes you selfish too. It is so overwhelming that there is no room left for something or someone else and again I go to my room and cry in shame, sorrow, guilt, despair. I pray to a heaven of brass for the strength and wisdom and love to be there, in all my brokenness for sure, to be able to at least give what I do have to my Love and to my other children.

Last Hours

I have to let her go. In my mind I use expressions I learned when I was young: we have to entrust her body to the earth from which God made her. Her life is God's. He made her. She belongs to Him and with Him she is safer than she would have ever been with me; more loved, cherished, protected.

How I would have liked to cooperate with God in His plan for her life and to be able to tell her about His goodness and grace. But she doesn't need that anymore. She already has everything. My arms and belly are empty, my breasts almost have no milk left, my tears seem to flow incessantly. The pit is deep. Physically I feel how I miss her.

I beg God to come into my sadness. The pain doesn't diminish, but I don't feel alone. The missing her is intense and yet there is peace as well. I know He lives and that I am loved, just like Amanda, and that I can just sit here, be, feel, cry. It is okay. It feels very important how I deal with this and what choices I make. I know I don't go through this for the rest of the world, yet I have a feeling that people are watching how we are and what we do in this situation. This also gives me strength somehow. I taste what I believe and discover there can be pain while you feel loved by God.

Today we have to bury Amanda. I feel miserable. When the children were tucked in yesterday, my Love and I watched movies and drank wine. We even laughed and relaxed a bit. That was nice, but we forgot that I am still a mother who has just given birth. The delivery seems far away, but my body now tells me that it is really only five days ago.

We had a good afternoon yesterday after all. We talked, prayed, laughed, cried. In the evening I asked all of the children to crawl in bed with me. We huddled together and talked about what will happen today. After that we sung the songs we will sing during the service. We really need and will need this: 'Strength will rise as we wait upon the Lord, we will wait upon the Lord, we will wait upon the Lord.' It is actually not a statement of faith, but more a cry out of desperation, a plea for faith. At this moment I don't sing because I believe it, but because I *want* to believe it.

How my heart hurts, how deep my crying goes. Amanda. I go to her again. She lays there before me. Just as peaceful. Completely herself. My belly cramps. The thought that she will go into a closed basket, makes me feel nauseous. I can't leave her behind, can I? I must. Cognitively I know: she cannot stay here, her body decays. There is a huge contrast between what I rationally know and emotionally feel. I consist of two persons.

The others are awake now too. The last hours with Amanda have begun. Emma comes in, together with another woman. It is the first time that a funeral has come this close to me and a dead person is carried out of my house. Emma asks who wants to be there when we lay Amanda down in the basket. One of the children wants to and the three of us go to her room and lay Amanda before us again. We watch her, take care of her. Then we cautiously lay her down in the white basket, we cover her with the white and pink blanket. I almost can't control myself. I want to wail and whine very very loudly, like an Eastern woman. I restrain myself. My Love and my children need me.

Now that we have taken care of her for the last time and she will stay in this position, I can more freely touch Amanda. I caress her body through the blanket. Desperately I keep stroking her while I walk with her to our bedroom. This is the last time I can do it. I rather don't want to share her with others, but I must be there for the children and I also want that, I somehow really *do* want to share it too. My daughter. Our daughter. Your sister. My hearts screams cries of despair to God while I try to restrain myself. I see the eyes of my children on me. I have to mirror how you deal with this but I don't know how to deal with this. Oh God, in silence I scream. Oh God.

I sit down on the edge of our bed and watch her a bit longer, attentive, while I caress and cherish my deceased girl. Then I place the basket in the middle of the bed and give each of us the opportunity to do what we want to do. We say goodbye, though we don't know how you do that. With the six of us we crawl around Amanda. Bye, sweet Amanda, we will see you later. We will see you again.

Emma takes pictures of our hands around the open basket. Then we put the white and pink lid on it. Two children tie the ribbons. Some more pictures. It's time, guys. We have to go. We go to the car for our first and last ride with the seven of us, as a complete family. We are going to bury our daughter and sister. I want drama: bells and whistles and a lot of attention. At the same time I want to sink deep into the ground. My life is over.

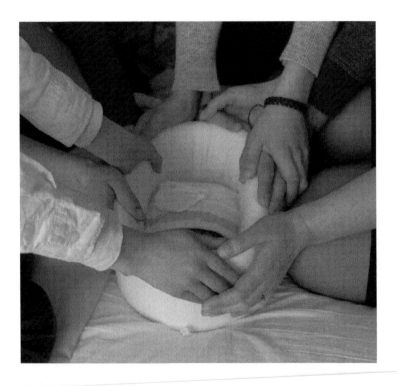

Handheld

We are the last ones to walk into the crowded auditorium where the memorial service is taking place. The song that carried us through the delivery sounds again: 'We are not alone. We are not alone for God is with us'. My Love carries his child and places the closed basket on the stage in front of the room. How different from those other times that he carried his baby into church to dedicate them to the Creator. It's preposterous. That big, strong, tough daddy with his little baby. Flesh of his flesh. I want to cry very loudly again but constrain myself. I so hope I manage to maintain this.

Philip, worship leader of our church and musician with whom I made music for years, leads the singing with his guitar. It is simple, familiar and good. I loudly sing along, as if by singing the words become true. As if by singing them very loudly, I can at least do something in this otherwise hopeless situation. I sing when others can't, even at the funeral of my own child. For a moment, I don't care what other people think of me. Or do I? I do constantly feel that I have to be an example. As if everyone is watching me and observing how I deal with the challenges I face, including this one.

I try to watch my children. Though we invited a lot of people so the children can talk with them about it later, there is no one who puts an arm around my children or around me. They probably also don't know what to do in a situation like this. I feel even more observed. As if I am on an island with my family and the rest are watching us. I feel very keenly that I have to show myself to be strong whilst I prefer to choose to be broken. But I am not going to withdraw from mothering my living children. Although I am also the mother of Amanda, who is laying there in her closed basket in front of the room, with candles around it and seven wooden stars: two big and five little ones. That's us.

During the service we switch places. Sometimes one child needs us, then another one. I wrestle with my own grief and my desire to be there for my family at the same time. I have the feeling I need to be there for the other guests as well and feel an enormous yoke on my shoulders. Who is looking after me? God, where are You? Two mourning parents and four mourning children. Who is helping whom? I can't tell. We do what we can, try not to drown in our own sadness while actually we are going under. Am I there for my children or do I cling to them? I continually pray short prayers: Give wisdom. Help. It hurts so much. What should I do? Lord! I try to follow my heart, because the Holy Spirit lives there, doesn't He?

The service is over. We have to go to the grave. Now I do cry almost uncontrollably and with everything inside of me

I try to contain myself. I don't know if I can stop when I let go. The pain is unbearable. I hold my Love. He carries our child. The youngest living children are rampageous. The tension comes out. They laugh and tease. I understand them, though it makes me feel uncomfortable as well. I choose to not take offence, to accept the situation as it is. We walk in a long procession to the grave. I want to look after my children, my Love, my parents, but I need all my strength to contain myself.

The weather is good and it is only a short walk. At the field where her grave is waiting, a tree is blossoming. The pink blossom makes a lovely and comforting setting for this pitch-black scene in our history. I hold Amanda on my lap for a while and feel a strong urge to act very dramatically. I resist it.

When everyone is gathered, my Love climbs via a ladder into the grave. When he is at the floor, I give Amanda to him. He looks up to me and I see my own emotions in his eyes. We are one. He lays our child on the cold ground and climbs out of the grave again. Wordless, we fall in each other's arms and firmly hold each other. Our tears fall together. Our child lies in her grave.

Together we speak out the Creed. A ritual I remember from earlier funerals that seemed important to me. To speak out what you hold on to although you feel or even believe nothing. Cody prays and then it is done. The guests walk past and sprinkle rose petals in the grave.

Amanda lies in her grave, sweetly covered in a basket with rose petals over it. The six of us stay behind. I have to make every effort to resist the urge to take her back out of the grave again. The children take their time to walk around a bit, to cry, look, hug. I walk little rounds around it. I want to get out of here. I don't know how long I can withhold myself. I want her back!

I can't leave her here alone, can I? What mother leaves her child alone in a ditch? I know this is how it should be and has to be. I just can't take her back home again. When we finally walk back to the car without our fifth child, I feel ripped apart and broken. I have also left myself, or at least a part of me, behind.

CONTRASTS

For condolences and a lunch we drive to the school building where our church gathers on Sundays. Most of the time I am not really there. I speak to some people, cry a little bit sometimes and furthermore try to withhold my tears as much as possible. I have the feeling I have to go back to normal, but actually I want to be buried myself.

I rationalize: I have children on both sides of eternity. Amanda does not need me; our living children need me. I find out it is impossible indeed to choose one child above another. I love all five of them, I want to take care of them all. Because I can't do anything anymore for Amanda, I choose the other four, but at the same time I feel sharply and poignantly that a part of me has died. I am an amputated mother.

We come home exhausted. The children are wild. We go outside to sit in the sun. The contrast between our inner and outer world couldn't have been greater. The children play and there are even other kids coming to play in our garden. All seems cosy and relaxed. We just buried our long-expected child and now we drink a beer in our garden. The father of one of the neighbour kids comes in and gives his condolences. We tell him today was the funeral. He doesn't know what to say. We don't either.

I want to wail and cry but I don't. Why? If this is the worst thing that can happen to you, as they say when someone's child dies, then isn't this the moment to wail and cry very loudly? We just don't know what to do and search for ways to express, feel and suppress and make life for the children as normal as possible. The ice-cream man comes. Yes, you may have an ice-cream. Why not. We live today. Apparently children can die. Who says these four are still here tomorrow? Let us enjoy what we have now.

With surprise we look at each other. We don't know ourselves anymore. We don't know each other anymore. We have to carefully pay attention, making sure we keep talking to each other, because apparently we need to get to know ourselves and each other all over again. More than that our child is gone, we also left our old self behind. We decide that, from now on and as long as needed, we will take a walk together every day to share what we think and feel, even though we sometimes do not understand each other.

It is late and time to go to bed. Yet once more I go to Amanda's room. Her scent is still there. Amanda is now also physically gone. We are the six of us again, without a happy expectation and without a baby. I weigh too much, despite giving birth. I need to lose weight but want to become pregnant again right away. Give us twins then Lord. Bless us double because of our loss. But it isn't wise right now. I want to make love, feel, touch. But it is not yet possible and besides that I have too much grief. Amanda is gone. Her soul is in heaven, her body lies in the ground. We have to move on, but I don't know how.

Every night we drink. Numb the pain, choose oblivion. But when the movie has ended and the bottle is empty, when it is really time to go to bed, the pain comes again with even greater force. It seems that it becomes worse every minute. I feel what writer Kristien Hemmerechts says: 'Parents should have the option to be buried together with their child.'[8] Continuing to live after the death of your child just doesn't make sense. That your body keeps on functioning despite carrying death inside you, having death in your hands. But I have more children! They are just as dear to me. I cannot leave them behind but I can't choose either. How can you choose with which child would you rather be? It is just impossible.

A few days later I wake up. My Love is getting himself dressed. I smile and want him to kiss us goodbye. A familiar and tender moment. Intimate happiness. But then all the sudden fear hits me. Us? Where is she? I feel next to me and realize I am not breastfeeding a child. The image was so real that I need some time to calm myself down again and grasp reality. My child is dead. Dead. Dead.

DisHEARTENEd

How do you move on with your life after you have buried your child? I get up, eat breakfast with the children, help them to get ready for school. I cannot take them there yet; I am still a woman who has newly given birth. Happily my Love is able to do the daily routines outside our home. I am barely capable of doing things inside our house.

Today it hurts more than yesterday. I resist the pool of sadness that wants to consume me, but I realize that somehow I have to go through this. I hoped that from now on it would become less hard. That the funeral would be the lowest point and from there it would only become better. But it turns out it doesn't work that way.

I still love her, although she has passed. I have motherly feelings: love that was born together with my fifth child but did not die together with her. This urge to take care and to cherish is especially for her and exists next to the love I have for my oldest, second, third and fourth child. I pray I can give this love to my other children, but it turns out that it seems not to work like that. Apparently my love is as unique as my children are. My love for Amanda doesn't erase my love for the others, but it doesn't amplify it either.

My heart has grown bigger, I think. Love has been added. Only I don't know where to go with it. My body tells me I gave birth recently. But there is no baby. This is what a widow meant in her post on Facebook: 'Grief is love with no place to go'.

Meanwhile I have four older children for whom I can and want to be there. I want to be involved with them and protect them from my endless deep sorrow, but I can't bring myself to do it. I rather want to be with Amanda or just watch futile videos so that I don't have to think about her. I feel like drowning, as if the ground has been cut from under my feet after all. Where I always had words, I now can't find them anymore. I don't know what I think, feel, believe or know. I am numb. My child lies in her grave. Her soul is with God and nothing can take her place. I sink away in emptiness and sadness. I lost a child and it is terrible. But God must be still there and I want to turn to Him now also. 'Lord, come in my sadness, my pain, this emptiness and show me that You are my comforter.'

Time goes on and so does life. I do not consciously think of Amanda every second but missing her is constantly present. I can't grasp it, I feel broken and live on autopilot. When I wake up, the first thing I see is Amanda. I know that I have to turn my eyes upon Jesus, but I don't know how you do that anymore. Maybe I should listen to the podcasts and songs people send me. I'm not looking forward to it, because I might have to cry. I would rather go and do something.

This morning I read the text from the memorial service again, 1 Corinthians 15. To reap a spiritual body, there always has to be something of flesh and blood first. It reassures me. Amanda had a body of flesh and blood, so she also has a spiritual body. She wasn't conceived in vain. I didn't suffer for her for nothing. She really is with Jesus. Although I would love to have her here, I am glad that it wasn't all for nothing.

Last week I barely prayed and hardly connected with God. But I can't handle this without Him. So I want to repent. I believe the songs we sang at the funeral. I know Jesus is alive. I run away in apathy so I don't have to fathom the deep darkness of this sorrow and pain. But it is the only way. To walk through the valley. To not run. To not sit down. To just walk.

I feel lonely and sad. Other people do not understand me. Some say literally: 'I can't do much for you, except pray.' That is what I need the most, I think, because I don't know how you do this: mourning, living with grief. I'm not taking good care of myself. I go to bed too late and don't pay attention to what I eat and drink. It is as if paying attention to me and my body focusses me more on Amanda. I still want to breastfeed her, hug her, hear her, smell her, but she is gone. She passed away and I don't know how to move on, so I just work hard or numb myself.

Just be Held

Every morning I get up and just read what *Our Daily Bread* says
I should read and try to get through the day. Today someone
texted me a song by Casting Crowns. It touches me deeply:

Hold it all together
Everybody needs you strong
But life hits you out of nowhere
and barely leaves you holding on

And when you're tired of fighting
Chained by your control
There's freedom in surrender
Lay it down and let it go

So when you're on your knees
And answers seem so far away
You're not alone
Stop holding on
And just be held

Your world's not falling apart
It's falling into place
I'm on the throne
stop holding on and just be held

Just be held, just be held. This is exactly what I feel: Everybody needs me strong. This song acknowledges that. It makes me feel seen. Life did hit me out of nowhere and barely leaves me holding on. Indeed. But that there is freedom in surrender, that I have to break the chains of wanting to keep everything under control... I don't want that yet. Besides: how do you do that: just be held? Anger and longing are fighting for the right of way in my heart, but I realize that at least it is true that He is on the throne.

In the words of Jerry Sittser, who lost his mother, wife and daughter in a car crash, I recognise the same experience: 'For months I was a broken man. I wasn't able to do anything for God and didn't feel like obeying him. Night after night I sat in the living room, not able to say anything, pray anything, or do anything. The only thing I was capable of was allowing God to love me, though I hardly believed He loved anyone and certainly not me. I had no idea how to believe and if I wanted to believe.'[9]

I decide to just speak it out: 'I want to be held, but I don't know how. It has become clear to me that I don't have control and as I have nowhere else to go, I allow You to take control then.'

WHERE is SHE?

Oh Amanda
Will I really never see you again?
Never feel you moving in my belly
Never softly sing to you
Cherish you while caressing you
Will I really never hear your voice
See your eyes look around?

It is as if a sword pierces my belly
A very loud NEVER rears its head
NEVER will I hold you again
NEVER will I see you again
NEVER will I hear your voice
Feel your fingers grasp
See your mouth seek

I cry and scream and whine miserably

Oh God. You have my child there do You?
Is she surely there, safe with You?
Now that I can't hug her, will You do that for me
Now that I can't give her my love, please show me ways to
express and give it out.
This mother's heart has more than it can give and
overflows with pain, love and sadness.

In my head Amanda has a chair at our dinner table, a room in our house. She has a permanent place in my heart no one and nothing else can take. The awareness that I lost a child, cuts in so deeply that I rather try to not let it sink in, but by not allowing it to sink in, I deny myself.

I read in a book that grief means working hard[10] and we both feel that. This grief also affects our children and might affect a new baby. It is inevitable and it is time that I realize that and accept the reality of my loss. I am so angry about it. This is not what I wanted for my children! I did not want to saddle them up with sadness and pain and loss, but to give them a brother or sister to love, to bond and play with. Instead of that there is a heaviness inside of me that my children feel as well. We are not a family of six and yet we are. We are a family of seven, but one is missing.

Actually I am completely lost. I, who always had lovely words when someone was suffering, even when someone died. I don't know anymore. What kind of place actually is that beautiful heaven? Are individuals really seen there? Is my daughter better off there then here with me, a mother who is watching her 24/7 or making sure someone else does that?

God, do You really see her? Are You really taking care of her or is she in some kind of nursery with hundreds of other babies and one nursing angel? The stories from children's Bibles aren't enough anymore. My mother's heart needs more than comforting songs. I had to hand in my child at an unknown location. With unknown caretakers, unknown schedules, and an unknown destination. I lost her in more than one way. Not only do I not see her anymore. I also don't know where she is. I, the stay-at-home mom who almost never brought her children to childcare, had to hand my child involuntarily in at an unfamiliar address.

I walk around for days like this. Bewildered. Searching. Where is she? I want to say to God: 'You can give her back now. She needs to be fed and to grow up. You can have her back after that. What are You doing with her anyway? Is she safe, happy?'

Some people sent me songs with lyrics like: 'Can You give her a hug from me?' And: 'Will You sing our songs to her?' At first I thought it was foolish, but now I feel the need also to know at a deeper level that she is really safe and protected.

One Saturday morning I realize I can't go on like this. I go to our bedroom again, lock the door, fall on my knees and pour out my heart. Finally I tell everything out loud to God. I have to know if she is seen, if she is taken care of, if she is really safe in the arms of her heavenly Father. When I'm done, I feel a little calmer and look forward to some kind of answer, a reassurance, a sign.

That afternoon with the mail there is a postcard from my sister. She tells me that she thinks of me and tells me what her daughter said: 'Joni wants me to say that God is taking really good care of Amanda.' When it sinks in, I cry: Amanda is seen and known. What we wrote on her birth card is really true: 'From mommy's belly straight into the arms of her heavenly father'. I sigh gratefully and am relieved. Amanda is safe.

Now I remember that moment a few weeks ago when I got the overwhelming realization that Theo really is in heaven. It is no make-believe, but reality. I didn't make it up. When I realized it that day, I was so happy and impressed. Heaven is real. There is life after death. That means Amanda is alive, just as Theo is. Maybe they are even together. I quiet my mother's heart.

A little later I read what Jesus says in John 14:27-28: 'Peace I leave with you; my peace I give you. I do not give to you as the world gives. Do not let your hearts be troubled and do not be afraid.' And: 'If you loved me, you would be glad that I am going to the Father, for the Father is greater than I.' Then I grasp that Amanda is with the Father too. I have to let her go. If I love her, I should rejoice because she is with the Lord. It will probably take a while before I am really able to do that but becoming aware of this seems an important first step to me.

Months later, my friend Abby tells me that she prayed a lot when I was giving birth to Amanda. She received an image from God. She saw me in the living room standing next to the cradle. Jesus stood by me and pointed outside, to the back yard. There was a paradise there. Such a beautiful, lovely garden. I cry while she tells me this and Abby says: 'The image I had seemed to tell me: Amanda is doing well.'

Picking up the Pieces

It's time to bring my children to school myself again. I don't look forward to it. What if everyone thinks that I am back to normal, while all I am doing is warily trying to step outside again? How can I explain that it seems grief is only getting worse every day? That every time I think I hit the bottom of the pit, that pit turns out to be even deeper?

I feel scalped. More naked than naked. Skinned I walk and bike through the street. It feels as if everybody sees directly what's wrong with me. I perceive everything without a filter. I don't have a layer of protection anymore, but I do have the feeling that everyone can see by looking at me: this woman buried her child. Grief not only is my companion, it is taking me over completely and takes my breath away. I recognize what writer A.F.Th. van der Heijden writes: 'We have lived with a strangling loss now for six weeks. That is not an empty metaphor. We experienced, and are experiencing every day, how a compelling absence can literally tighten your throat with her tentacles. The scream gets stuck in the throttle. Loss is a strangler who doesn't grant its victim much more than some gurgling.'[11]

At school people ask me how I am doing. A mother tells me that I just need to quickly have another baby. An older teacher tells me in tears that sixteen years ago she also lost a child. A mother is happy to see me again and in the supermarket I meet another mother who thinks it's brave of me to do things and tells me she read an article in a women's magazine about Emma, our undertaker. Everyone has their own response. Exhausted I come home. This adds to it all. You not only have to figure out how to live with this hole in your heart, you also have to learn to deal with how other people respond to your disaster.

I call a friend. She says I'm allowed to do this my own way. I find out more and more how sad I am and that it is really about *her* and not about the loss of 'a' baby. Maybe I will receive another child in the future. But Amanda isn't coming back and that loss will always be there. It makes me angry and plunges me even deeper into the valley.

My Love says to me: 'This will always be a part of our life. When we are old, we will still think of her and miss her.' I feel resistance to those words. Will this really rule our entire life? I want to believe God for healing and restoration of our hearts. But I also know that I have to learn to accept that this has impacted our lives and changed them indeed. We had a baby. Her name is Amanda. She doesn't live anymore.

My sister directs a musical and I go to watch it with my eldest children. A huge step: going out with a hole in your heart. In the underground I meet a woman who I have fond memories of. She asks me how many children I have.

Hesitantly I tell her I have five children. She asks about the age of the youngest. I feel very uncomfortable with my eldest near me and the grief about my youngest suddenly very severely popping up. It still hasn't sunk in with me. I tell her what happened and hope my children forgive me for crying.

I have to move on with my life and be there for the other children. I don't want them to suffer more than they already do because of what has happened in our family. But my life is on hold while the rest of the world keeps turning. My life has totally changed while from the outside all looks the same. I don't know how to go on and decide to at least keep on doing the daily things. Getting up in the morning. Reading my Bible, praying, having breakfast with my children, coaching them in their daily tasks, preparing meals, washing and cleaning.

Our family counsellor asks me if I am also slowly getting back to work, as my Love is doing. I tell him I don't dare to play the piano yet. But he didn't refer to my song writing, but to my role in tutoring my older child, which I receive a personal budget for. He says I should take that up slowly as well. I do not have to function at a high level immediately. That comes to me. In my head, I already have to function fully normally again, but that I am by trial and error keeping the house up and running, is good progress already. The rest will come.

Choices

We go on vacation together with the family I grew up in which now consists of thirty-eight persons. It was already planned and we decide to go because of the children. I am really dreading it. I am not a people person and now that I don't know how to mourn and if I am allowed to mourn, I do not feel at ease. Besides that, I have a constant feeling that everyone is watching how I do this.

I need something to help me to give Amanda and my grief a place here, so I decide to place some cards we received, photos and the birth card in our holiday room. It becomes a kind of mourning room, although it is holiday. You can't take a break from grief. Still I wonder if I am exaggerating. I search for a form, a way to justify Amanda, our living children, ourselves and God. I would like someone to tell me what I am doing well and who would, if necessary, lovingly tell me how I might do it otherwise.

In a book by Max Lucado, I read: 'When life is bad, you will be tempted to forget God. Enticements will come, but don't do dumb or stupid things. Make choices that please God.'[12]

He mentions Joseph and how he again and again had a choice in how to live, in what he did with what he experienced. That choice I have as well. I can thank God for what I have and serve Him with what I have. Amanda is His and so are we. I decide I keep trying to stay close to God and to see what will happen.

It is very hard. Grief keeps coming up. It is really very bad that Amanda died. I want to believe that God will lead me through this and focus on Him and His word. But I tend to comfort myself with the wrong things, such as food and alcohol. I sink away in loneliness. A bastion wherein I also don't allow my Love. That is not how it should be. I seek for support and comfort. Comfort God can give but I can't receive. Comfort I maybe don't *want* to receive.

I think I am going to sing again. I go through my folder of songs. As a worship leader I collected a lot of them. There is not much I can sing with my heart. Even the songs I wrote myself, I can't get out of my throat: 'Nothing is wasted with God. Nothing is wasted by God. Thank you, Lord, You keep us in peace…' Well no, not really. Though I am not completely desperate, I don't feel like singing that with God everything is well in the end. I even do not really want that. I don't want God to make something beautiful out of this. I don't accept my fate. I just want my child back.

In the end I sing the song I sent to Theo's widower and others send to me: 'Still, my soul, be still'. To me, it's more a prayer than a statement. I hope it is true that 'the darkest night disappears when daylight breaks through.'[13] I wonder if that will ever happen. But it is a good song. Still, my soul, be still. Wait for the Lord. You don't feel anything now. You are broken. You are grieving for your child. You are worried about your other children. It is okay. It will be well. One day you will see Amanda again and all relationships will be restored.

So I just keep on singing songs, writing, reading the Bible. My soul appears to be deaf and blind. It doesn't sink in, but I keep on doing it. I don't feel anything and do not have any sense that I hear God's voice, but I want to keep focusing on Him and honour Him. I choose to position myself where I *might* hear God's voice, in case He wants to say something.

A mother who also lost her fifth child, emails me and says that in her head she is doing everything she does also for her deceased daughter. In the beginning, it seemed a bit overdone to me, but now I realize I include Amanda in everything. She is a part of me, and that part is gone now. Just as I feel it in my body when something is wrong with my older child, I also feel it in my body that Amanda is not there anymore. I feel a deep need to express that in some way. But I don't know how. I'm in pain and I am very sad. I see my nephew Brian. He lays in the playpen and I think of Amanda who will never lay in a playpen. How I miss her and the prospects of dreaming of how she will be, how she will become. When I take a walk with my Love a little bit later, he says he is wandering and I understand. I think it is special that we can be together without feeling and thinking exactly the same per se.

Do what Feels Right?

Words are important to me, but I often can't find words for what I feel or think. Reading books depicting what we go through and what to expect, helps. In many of those books William Worden's model is mentioned. According to this model I need to do the following:

1. Accept the reality of the loss
2. Live through the pain and the sorrow
3. Adjust to a new life wherein the deceased person isn't present anymore
4. Find a continuous connection with the deceased while getting back to life at the same time

In those same books they say there is no manual for how to do this. Everyone has to complete these tasks in their own way and there is no right or wrong in grief. You have to do what feels right. To be honest, I think that's rubbish. One of the first things I thought when we found out that Amanda had really died, was: 'I need a cigarette'. I wanted to smoke again. Later that night I wanted whiskey and cigars and there are more things you can't truly call 'right' even when you're overwhelmed by grief.

Some believing women who lost babies as well show me that you can live on after such a great loss and that you can keep your faith while missing a child. 'Step by step, Ineke', they say. This is not something you fix in a few months, but every day is a day.

It helps to think this way, it makes this a little bit better to handle. I'm reminded of what Brian Doerksen shared about lament in a songwriting workshop. He said it is so important to lament. You also find it in the Bible. I decide that in the coming weeks I will mainly read the Psalms and Job. I observe that that is very good for me.

Somewhat later I read in a book by Manu Keirse – one of the best-read authors on grief in my language: 'It's not necessarily going to get better as time goes by. To say that would not only be untrue, but also inappropriate. When people are dealing with grief, they have days that are better than others. On some days the pain of the loss will strike in full force. [...] It is important to keep in mind that with this pain also comes healing. One has to live from day to day and try to get through this day.'[14]

I am cold and decide to go out for a walk. I wander around, as my soul wanders, searching for new ground and meaning in this landscape of grief and sadness. Just now I almost fell because of the holes in the grass next to the canal. It made me think of a line in the musical *Les Misérables*: 'I stumble and I fall'. Both Jean Valjean and Javert sing a little bit later: 'I escape now from this world of Jean Valjean'. Jean

Valjean means that he leaves behind a life of stealing and the stigma of being an ex-prisoner: he embraces the life the priest is offering him. Javert means that he rejects the grace Valjean is offering him: he would rather die. Jean Valjean finds life. Javert kills himself eventually.

I believe I have a similar choice in how I respond to suffering and death. I do stumble. I do sometimes fall almost too (literally some moments ago). I miss Amanda and I am sad my children are confronted with such a loss. So: 'I stumble and I fall', but: 'I escape now from this world'. I am sad, but I refuse to drown in this sadness, though to do just that is very appealing sometimes. I chose to give my sadness to God over and over again (although I don't always get how to do that exactly). I choose to trust I will come through this, whatever that means. I keep wandering and I keep writing to organize my thoughts. And I keep trying to allow my tears to come once in a while and pray I will better understand and embrace this.

Walking

Almost every day I walk the same path around the golf course behind our neighbourhood. Today it is a slippery road. I walk alongside the water and the wind is wild, the clouds are grey. Soon it will start to rain. It is just what I need right now. Cold wind, drizzly rain, splashing water and a muddy path on which I have to walk carefully so I won't slide. My life feels the same.

I plod through the mud and make sure I don't fall, slip, or sink away. I walk and ponder. My tired feet teach me that this day will pass. Just as my feet continue to walk over muddy places, uneven paths, through sudden gusts of wind or unexpected warmth, so my life also goes on. Breathe in, breathe out. From one situation into another and everything comes to an end. Just as my walk ends.

Life in the Bible often is compared to a road you travel, and I remember Hopes' words when we were in the hospital: 'You have to walk through the valley. Not sit in it. Not run through it. Just walk.' It gives me some support in this valley full of Amanda's death, that turns out to be a valley indeed. In the hospital it seemed so obvious that there would be an end to this, but now it doesn't anymore. It feels like an endless survival tour now without a finish in sight.

But just as my walk always ends, there also will come an end to seasons and periods in life. Just as I probably will walk again tomorrow, I will also have new adventures in my life. In the many books and articles I read about grief, one sentence hit me especially hard: 'Our life is a sequence of losses. It is indeed more extraordinary when life is calm than when it is full of crises.' The loss of my daughter is not the only loss I have suffered and there will be new losses in the future. Loss is something everyone has to learn to live with.

Just as I walk literally, I walk out my grief figuratively. They say grief never disappears completely but I hope that over time it will become more woven into who I am and that it will be like my physical walk: the path takes me along mud and mess and obstacles, but also along beautiful views, gentle breezes and moments of awareness that I don't have to do it alone and that this will come to an end.

WHERE is God?

Mourning time is over. At least, that is what we said to each other: Let us at least not take up new tasks in the first six weeks or try for another pregnancy. We will just grieve.

Now that time has passed. But sadness and missing her appear not to have passed. So maybe now it is just the time to clear up a bit and to carefully try doing some new things. We received a lot of postcards. It is so heart-warming. Over time I placed them everywhere in our living room and I think clearing them is a good way to start. While picking up the cards, I feel resistance. Apparently, I realize, this is too soon. In this case 'do what feels right' seems to be a good advice after all. I put the cards back in a different fashion. They are not everywhere in the room now, but all on one place. Grief is not coming at us from every corner of the room anymore.

Grief still seems only to be getting worse instead of less. I didn't expect that. Every time I think 'now I have cried enough', new tears come and again the bottom of the pit isn't there yet. Sittser writes that as well: 'The first torrent of loss slowly gave way to a steadily forcing pain in the months that followed. Just as water finds every way it can go, sorrow enters and scrapes every crack of the human mind. I thought I was going crazy. I became very depressed. It seemed the foundation of my life threatened to collapse.'[15]

I keep doing my daily tasks, continually aware of the four sets of eyes that are watching me. I want to be an example to my children and hold onto my faith, but God feels miles away. I try to stay honest and open, but often my thoughts are so dark that I don't dare tell anyone. So I watch videos. Numb the pain.

When I share with my Love that I don't know if I still believe and I can't do anything with what Christians tell me, he says: 'I keep looking to what happened in the past. You were in a wheelchair and you've been healed. We experienced other miracles and have noticed God was there. So now I just choose to believe and in about three years I will look further.' I am a bit surprised by what he says but very encouraged most of all. He doesn't know either, but he makes a choice. I could try to do that too. Yes, I am going to try that.

My friend Joy texts me: 'Don't forget in the dark what you heard in the light'. I feel offended and ashamed. Offended, because I feel misunderstood in my grief. Yet I know Joy and I watched her mourn her parents. I know she doesn't deny my sadness. And ashamed, because I know she's right. Actually it comes down to what my Love said already.

Still I often wonder how other Christians do this. I heard people share that they experienced misery, went through it and when it was over, they had a stronger faith and grew in intimacy with God. But how did they actually do that? Many months later I read what I needed to read now. In a book of one of my big role models, C.S. Lewis, I read how he felt when he mourned his wife.

'Meanwhile, where is God? This is one of the most disquieting symptoms. [...] But go to Him when your need is desperate, when all other help is vain, and what do you find? A door slammed in your face, and a sound of bolting and double bolting on the inside. After that, silence. You may as well turn away. The longer you wait, the more emphatic the silence will become. There are no lights in the windows. It might be an empty house. Was it ever inhabited? It seemed so once.'[16]

So I am not the only one to whom heaven seems sealed, apparently. It doesn't mean He isn't there, but I just don't detect it. My Love agrees with me when he says: 'People expect you to believe and know God is there and they include feelings in that knowledge. But that is exactly what is painfully mismatched. God probably is here, but I don't detect it.'

Rituals

I don't recognise myself anymore. I became someone else and I need to relate anew to the world, my family and myself. I still feel scalped when I walk down the street. It is as if everyone can see me to the core and verify the horrible terrifying reality just by looking at me: her child died. She has been a grave.

Things I never expected I would do or want, I now do or want. I go to the grave regularly, for example. I used to think a grave didn't matter, because there only lies a soulless body. Now I passionately bike there, walk to her spot, make it neat and take a big detour home. I don't know how to handle my emotions, as they are feelings I never had before. By biking fervently I can let go of some of them. I want to take care of my child and because that is impossible, I take care of the place where her body lies.

I feel jealous when I see ducks with chicks and goats with young. With surprise I wonder if I'm going crazy. Guarded, I ask other bereaved parents about it and am relieved to hear that there are others who struggle dealing with spring and all manifestations of successful fertility. I especially envy that particular swan. Why is she allowed to parade with her five chicks? Why do I only have four left?

I want a tattoo. I want to show on the outside what is missing on the inside, to compensate my loss and maybe also claim the attention I would otherwise have had with my baby in a stroller. I think it's weird. I used to be against tattoos before, so I decide to put this longing on hold for now. In my state you shouldn't make irreversible choices. I buy beads with the letters of her name and make a bracelet with them. I wear it, a little bit ashamed but mostly proud. When I read somewhere that people in the past wore mourning bands, I understand this is my mourning band. I use it to show my child may have been buried but punched a gaping hole in my heart and life.

I remember what Cody, the elder who spoke in the memorial service, told us about rituals. He said that people often speak with disdain about them, but that rituals are more important than you might think. They support and can help express feelings and thoughts where there are no words. Especially if you don't have words, it helps to burn a candle, speak out a written prayer, perform a certain act.

I think that my need to go to the grave is also a kind of ritual, as is burning a candle in a Catholic church. I used to think it's strange when people do that, but now we always light a candle in remembrance of our daughter when we visit a church like that. It feels good. It makes visible and tangible what is unspeakable. It is good for my soul and for our family.

I keep searching for words too. First in the WhatsApp group, later on Facebook and eventually I decide to start a blog.[8] By writing I organize my thoughts, I figure out what I really feel and think. By sharing these in a blogpost, I create space where it can just be there. Then I can also cry about it. There were times when I read my blog over and over again, just until it didn't make me cry anymore when reading it. By doing this I begin to accept that things are different than I expected and that this is who I am now apparently.

---

[8] www.brokenbutreal.com, I've translated a lot of the content to English. You can find that on: www.walkthroughgrief.word press.com

Sometimes Your Grief Is Too Big

I am invited to go to a friend's wedding. I don't feel like it, but I go anyway because I care a lot about her and together we prayed for this day. Thankfully, someone from church gives me a ride. I just surrender to what comes my way. In church I sit between happy people who loudly and cheerfully sing beautiful songs. Songs that make me doubt if I am a Christian. I cry. No one in this crowded church notices. I am glad when the service finally is over and I go to find the person who gave me a ride. I can't explain that I feel terrible. In silence we drive to the reception.

When I step out of the car I see Ian and Livine, people I trust and have known for years. I cling onto them and cry uncontrollably. They lead me in and talk with me for almost an hour. I wonder if I am taking too much of their time and why they, at a wedding, give me so much time. I am ashamed that I can't stop crying. But at the same time I want to kiss them, I am so grateful that they take the time, pay me attention and even say helpful things.

'O Ineke', Livine says at some point: 'Sometimes your grief is so big you just can't feel anything else.' I look up at her, surprised. I allow her words to sink in deeply, like a medicine in my veins so saturated with that grief. I feel some hope. What she says implies to me that this is temporary, that a time will come wherein I *can* feel something else, although for sure now that isn't the case. I repeat and repeat and ruminate this sentence. It will come. Not now, but someday you will feel other things. Your grief is just too big right now.

Around this time the social worker calls me to ask how we are doing and if we need anything. I tell her that we so want to help the children but don't know how. She suggests we come to the memorial service in the hospital. My Love writes this about it in the WhatsApp group:

'Today we went with the children to a memorial service at the hospital wherein all children who died in the hospital that year are remembered. The social worker thought it was too soon for us, but because we are worried about the bereavement process of the children it seemed good for them to go. It was hard and emotional. There were about fifty other parents. The names of all the children were read out loud and we could place a rose in a vase. 'Life has changed and only after one year have you made a first circle' is how the family counsellor described it. 'After that year you've experienced everything for the first time without Amanda.' We are now still walking through life feeling clueless and without much energy or interest in anything. We live, we

113

are here. How we are doing? I have no clue, I really don't. This is unknown territory for us and I don't know if we are okay or not. Who decides that? We are. That is what it is. Tired, done and also dazed. We thought we knew by now how life works and who we are. That idea is really gone. If you lose your foundation like this, it is hard to point out what the consequences are. It is so elusive but in everything it's there. If something happens you know: this is how in the past I would have viewed or thought about that. We knew how to deal with things or had an opinion. But that is all gone now. We experience things completely different and we have to figure life out all over again. And besides that, we don't know if we're doing it the right way. I am still processing that it is this basic and deep. Maybe after a year I can say: "Oh, that is how you do it, just as last time."'

Why?

I should have had more faith, speak life more often, bless my baby more, break the doubts and negativity of other people in the name of Jesus. And I should have gone to hospital earlier.

I feel responsible for the death of my child. Although I did bless and pray, visited mainly the people who encouraged me and did call the hospital several times, still our child died. Is that God's will? Is it bad luck? Is it a result of living in a sinful world? Different people say different things.

Feeling guilty doesn't help me further in this process, although someone points out to me that feeling guilty sprouts from love: you wanted it better and nicer. It doesn't bring Amanda back to me. It also doesn't reduce the pain of missing her. But because we would love to have another child, I want to know what I could have done differently. Guardedly, I talk with a friend about this. She appears to have thought about this as well and she too struggles with why Amanda died. I am so relieved and glad I am not the only one.

What should I do with those feelings of guilt? I remember how someone once explained to me there is a difference between accusing and convincing. The devil accuses and tries to make people feel guilty without an escape. The Holy Spirit convinces us of sin: He shows what was wrong and points to Jesus, to forgiveness. I think I have to try to ignore the feelings of guilt and assume that if I did something wrong, God will show it to me.

But thinking like this also doesn't bring Amanda back. Amanda is and stays deceased.

Cody visits us again. I am so grateful that he allows us to talk and makes the effort to listen to us. He asks good questions and we can both talk about what happened, what we feel and think. I dare not to ask the why-question, but happily Cody starts to talk about that himself when he states that the answer to 'Why?' doesn't help. You can't do anything with the answer to that question. 'What really matters', he says, 'is: do you still trust God?'

Now he has my full attention. This is exactly what I ask myself. Do I still trust God? All the time I try to surrender everything to God and to trust Him. But I do not know anymore how you do that and if I am still able to. I am so angry about what has happened. I think I blame God for it and that I can pray whatever I want, but it doesn't make any difference. There are no guarantees. It could happen again, just like that.

So, is this what I needed God for then? To guarantee everything is going to be all right? But apparently we don't know what life will bring and what God will do. Children can die.

It is hard to have no answers. God is good, but Amanda died. God comforts me and helps me and gives rest, but Amanda died. Some women I got to know have lost three children. One woman expects another baby and the ultrasound showed deficiencies again. How can I help, encourage and comfort them and lead them to God's heart? If I am honest, I attribute it to Him also. But maybe I don't need to have all the answers. I should just be honest to them, and stay humble and respectful to God as well, I think.

When I talk with Barbara about this, she says: 'God is bigger, a mystery. Focus on His unchangeable character instead on what is happening. God is here. Acknowledge your faith that He is here and speak out what you feel, that you feel so alone. Ask God to show Himself to you.' I think I am going to try that.

A little later I read in *Our Daily Bread* about Gideon. Gideon asks God why in the past seven years He didn't do anything. The answer he gets is: 'Go in the strength you have. I am with you.' He doesn't receive any answer to the why-question. And we usually also don't. But He is with us and although it takes quite some time before I am willing to acknowledge it, it is exactly what I heard and discovered in the past months.

Amputation

I've read Job twice now, with a completely different mindset. I used to read it as a story about someone who is very ill, as I was. I identified the groaning of physical pain. But now I see the father who mourns his children. I feel the pain of losing a child. Pain I now know all too well. Pain that is still indescribable.

I am now reading the Psalms and I am grateful that, as in Job, there are so many exclamations of despair. So that is allowed: to express your pain, your raw complaints: 'God? Where are you?' To throw all your misery at the feet of your Creator. He can handle it. He doesn't feel threatened or offended by my emotions.

I once started writing a song about this, which translated says: 'With You I am safe, I can calmly breathe. I can just be myself, I don't need to pretend. With You.' I didn't finish writing it then, but I was reminded of the melody when I was reading the Psalms and I decide to complete the song.[9] How important it is to go to God with all your pain, anger, bitterness and misery. I am so angry about what has happened, although I do have more peace now because Amanda is doing well, and that is what I want the most. But also something has been ripped off, something in my heart is damaged seemingly beyond repair.

In Psalm 116:15 I read: 'Precious in the sight of the Lord is the death of His fondlings.' (My translation from the Dutch Bible I use). Amanda is God's fondling as He knew her before I knew she existed and He carries her, and me. I miss my little girl. But I also want to live on, in faith and in trust that she is doing well. Lord, touch me please. My heart is frosty and cold and so still. I almost don't feel anything. I want to numb myself and still also want to have faith. But how?

They say time heals all wounds, but that is not my experience yet. Still my grief seems to become bigger instead of smaller and a little bit desperate I ask a sweet lady from church, who buried her newborn son ten years ago: 'Will it ever become less? This deep, sharp pain?' While I say it, I point to a place near my heart and she points to exactly the same place on her body and says: 'No, it still hurts so much. Maybe God doesn't take away the pain, but He does go His way with it.'

---

[9] The original lyrics are: 'Bij U ben ik veilig, kan ik rustig ademhalen; kan ik gewoon mezelf zijn, hoef me niet beter voor te doen, bij U.'

This answer troubles me. I talk with my Love about it: 'I actually thought this would be something like breaking your arm. It hurts a lot and then, after it is set and a cast has been placed, it lingers for a couple of days, but then it heals and the bone becomes often stronger than before. It doesn't feel that way at all. I actually always miss her. She is not upfront, but in the background, so presently absent.' 'Yes', my Love says. 'You shouldn't compare it with breaking your arm but with amputation.'

Now, I didn't go through physical amputation myself. I imagine that when your arm has been removed, you can live on, but are confronted with your loss every day. You can function, you are creative, you find ways to compensate your missing arm, but you do feel the loss; you see others with two functioning arms, which makes you feel jealous sometimes and you would want to just go back playing the piano or guitar, cooking, playing tennis or whatever you see people do with two arms. And sometimes, when the weather has changed, or some memories pop up, or when you bump into another person or a kitchen cabinet, you also feel the pain physically. Just as painful as in the beginning.

If this is what it is like, then the loss of our little girl indeed feels like amputation. I learn to live with it. I can function. I enjoy some moments purposely with more intensity because I know how fragile life is. But that deep sharp pain isn't gone and at unsolicited times it pops up again. I think I need to do then just what the Psalmists did: cry out to God. Being honest about what I feel and at the same time proclaiming what I do know deep down in my heart, even though still grumblingly and hesitantly: 'You are perfect in all of Your ways'.

Or, as they asked me to sing at a wedding lately: 'Lord, I want to praise Your love, even though my soul does not understand You. Blessed is he who dares to believe, even when the eye does not see. If your ways seem dark to me, I don't ask: why? One day I will see all Your splendour, when I get to Your heaven!'[10] With this sidenote: I do ask why, because I read that Job does that and David does that, and because I have this question in my heart and I want to stay honest. But still, this entrusting to God, though I don't understand at all, is only possible if I believe that His way in the end is the best.

Life is far from perfect, and my life is damaged, broken and crooked. But if His ways are perfect, then they lead somewhere. And then it is really true what I wrote in my song: I am safe with you, I can calmly breathe. So I read one more Psalm and feel the pain and the joy and remember that this is what makes me human. 'Broken but real' with an anchor in the God who is perfect in His way with me, although it doesn't feel like that at all.

---

[10] This is a Dutch song. The original lyrics are: 'Heer ik wil Uw liefde loven, al begrijpt mijn ziel U niet. Zalig hij, die durft geloven, ook wanneer het oog niet ziet. Schijnen mij Uw wegen duister, zie ik vraag U niet: waarom? Eenmaal zie ik al Uw luister, als ik in Uw hemel kom!'

This statue is made by Albert György and placed in Switzerland, at the Lake of Genève.

It was posted on various Facebook pages because of 'bereaved parents' month'. It touched me deeply.

PANIC

If one child can die, they all can die. I, and my Love as well, have lost confidence that everything is going to be all right. I recognize what Suzan Hilhorst writes about her deceased daughter Sara: 'Sara's story is the painful evidence of our transience. Neglectful, it has thrown all our certainties on the pyre and mercilessly put it on fire. The anonymous death we successfully ignore each day when we go to work, our family or the supermarket: she gave it a name, carefully pulled it out of the clay and made it visible again. Whether we like it or not.'[17] That is also becoming painfully clear to us.

When the ice cream man comes by, we now buy an ice cream. We never did that. We have pizzas delivered more often or get döner burgers. We used to think it was a waste of money, but now we think: who says it is still possible tomorrow? Let's give them what we can today. It takes us months before we find some balance again. We like the fact that we are a bit looser and become more generous, but it is not fun to no longer assume that we will be all alive and well today. 'The obviousness is gone', my Love says and that's exactly it. It makes us more grateful and generous, but it also regularly makes us feel insecure and scared.

I still feel Amanda moving in my belly. That's impossible of course, but she is still there. Our family seems too small now and often I am confused. I count and think a child is not there and feel the stress that comes with that. I think I exaggerate, but it happens unconsciously. We are going to eat and I call the children. They sit at the table and I look and feel unrest, some kind of panic: something is wrong. I wonder what it might be and then realize that I feel we are incomplete. I calm myself down, count them and then I find out that I have unconsciously counted Amanda too. Everyone is there. Well, everyone alive is there.

Time after time, this happens. We go somewhere, I check if everyone is there and I feel panic. I count and find out: I counted Amanda too. I feel ashamed about this, as she wasn't even born when she died. Do I have a right to feel this? But I can't help it. I don't do it on purpose. We are not a family of six anymore. We are a family of seven minus one. It is pointless to pretend we are not. It is the case and I have to learn to live with that.

When I wave my daughters goodbye, I feel my heart squeeze. It is such a delight to see those two frolic together, being children and becoming women. This feeling of happiness though comes with a dark shadow. There are three girls, but one I will never wave goodbye to. I just imagine she is there too. She is part of the cloud of witnesses[18] and because of that I assume she can see what happens here. I think it is not that bad if I pretend Amanda is with my other daughters when they go out together. I can't allow the grief about them not being complete rob me from the happiness that my daughters get along so well, can I? I want joy in, or despite, the missing.

When a child cries or screams, I am immediately very scared that something bad has happened. My heart beats faster, I jump up to see what is going on, and at the same time I silently calm myself down, so I can respond calmly to the children. That works well, but it makes me feel very insecure and it costs a lot of energy. I go to my general practitioner. I have to know if this is normal and if I mourn well. Again I hear that everyone mourns in their own way and that in mourning there is no right or wrong. I find that difficult. I have no clue how to mourn my own way. I have feelings I never had before and don't know how to deal with and I want to take good care of my family.

The general practitioner doesn't see signs of depression and is not worried. He suggests I could go to the 'Life Questions Consultant' and I decide to do that. For the sake of the children, because something I read disturbed me deeply: 'When parents lose a child, the remaining children not only lose their sibling, but often also mentally and emotionally the parents, and the family feeling, and the structures within which they felt safe. The parents go down in their own grief.' I so want to do this properly. I haven't been able to protect my children from grief and loss. But maybe I can protect them from emotional neglect by a grieving mother.

The consultant says I already did a lot of work. As long as the panic doesn't influence the way I function in normal life, my grief is not 'complicated grief'. It doesn't really help, what she says. So I toil on and keep calming myself down again and again. In the months following, the panic keeps coming back and even grows worse. My family doesn't suffer from it, but I do. Regularly I run outside for nothing, hearing a child scream and thinking one of my children had some kind of terrible accident. It makes me tired and anxious. When we are on holiday, two years after Amanda's death, and I'm panicked again and again, whenever a child cries – there were a lot of them on the campsite – I have had enough of it.

When I am home, I go back to the general practitioner and he says there must be more going on than mourning alone. He refers me to a psychologist who diagnoses me with posttraumatic stress disorder and proposes EMDR.[19] I discover that Amanda's death brought up deeper fears in me of when I was still a little girl, alone in the hospital. It is a severe treatment, but it helps. I have less panic attacks and a summer later I am way more relaxed on holiday. I can hear children cry without stressing out. Sometimes counsellors and God join hands, an elderly wise woman once said, and I am grateful that psychologists and treatments exist.

God Cries With Us

Sometimes people say or write: 'God cries with you'. I am reluctant to say something about this. As if I just don't *want* to let that sink in. Herb Vander Lugt writes, in a little leaflet from *Our Daily Bread* entitled *Why Christians doubt*[20]: 'I've concluded that many birth accidents and other abnormalities take place because we live in a world that has been broken and plagued by laws of natural consequence. I'm convinced that God doesn't directly cause birth defects, inherited imperfections, crippling diseases, or debilitating accidents. Instead, I believe He allows His spiritual enemy and the inherited consequences of sin to touch all of our lives in different ways. A child born into a Christian home, but who has genetic disposition to diabetes, for instance, seems to have the same statistical chance to develop this disease as one born into a family of atheists. It might seem that such natural law would rule out God's presence and involvement in a troubled world. But the Bible makes it clear that God remains in ultimate control of the world, even though He is never the source of evil. He enters with us into our plight. He grieves over pain.'

God grieves over pain. While He could also take it away, couldn't He? I find this very hard to understand and to believe. Still it is true that Jesus in so many ways bore the same burdens His suffering creatures are bearing. In the words of Isaiah 63:9 ESV: 'And he became their Saviour. In all their affliction he was afflicted, and the angel of his presence saved them; in his love and in his pity he redeemed them; he lifted them up and carried them all the days of old.' Vander Lugt then says: 'For those who trust Him, He is there to use our pain to make us better people (Romans 5:1-5) and to bring good out of our most distressing circumstances. (Romans 8:28)'

'You never cry alone', Ann Voskamp writes as well: 'Who can know why God allows your heart to break, but still the answer must be important enough because God allowed His heart to break too.'[21] I can't grasp it but still I think it is true. I don't understand what is happening. Why people have to go through terrible losses, treatments or procedures. That we lost our child. But I do not cry alone. It is a peculiar way of comfort. You would want the situation to change, the relation restored, the disease or behaviour disorder to disappear, the child to live again. But often that doesn't happen.

Maybe Jesus didn't come to make our lives easier in the first place, but to live among us, to help us bear. He suffered immensely Himself. God lost His own child. He understands us. He knows us. In the Bible I read God put our tears in a bottle. No tear falls unnoticed. I must say this is comforting to me. And in that sense this is already true: you never cry alone.

Some years ago I joined a 24/7 prayer event. I booked to pray for an hour and arrived in a lovely room that was decorated with posters and post-its on the wall, books on small tables and comfortable pillows on the floor. There was a guitar, a music stand and sheet music. Really a place to leave the world behind you and to focus on God completely.

I prayerfully read the prayer points that were posted on the wall and felt a bit depressed. So much need. So much sorrow. So much suffering. While praying and reading, I remembered that verse in the Bible about tears God is putting in a bottle. It's in Psalms 56:8 ESV: 'You have kept count of my tossings; put my tears in your bottle. Are they not in your book?' I pondered about it and asked: 'Lord, when those tears are in that bottle, then what? What do you actually do with them?' I felt as if He was answering in my thoughts: 'I drank them'.

I was astonished and filled with awe and disgust at the same time. Did God drink my tears? Are my tears part of the cup Jesus was wrestling with in Gethsemane, the cup He didn't want, but still drank, because it was God's will?

It's not literally said in the Bible, that Jesus drank our tears. But it does say that Jesus suffered because of our sins, our pain and our rejection. That is why I think I can say this: The cup Jesus was suffering for, wasn't only filled with our sins, but also with our tears. Even our tears of sadness, guilt, shame, anger, Jesus drank, bore.

So I don't cry alone. I also don't cry for nothing.

When Nothing Beats Anymore

Every year we go to the 'Vrij Zijn Zomerweek', a Dutch Christian summer conference. We didn't plan to go there this time, because we would have a baby. Now we do go, because the baby died. I find it very hard to be there and at first I skip the services and go into the woods instead, to write and to cry.

After some days I decide to go anyway. I deliberately arrive too late and choose a place in the back. I hope the songs will not be too happy. When the band starts to sing, I wait and see. To my surprise I find I can sing these songs along pretty well. The lyrics don't ignore or step over feelings and they don't pretend everything is all right as long as you have Jesus. There even are lines painfully pinpointing why this is so hard for me. Such as this one: 'Als er niets meer klopt, klopt het hart van God. God die overwint, Hij is met ons. Dus laat de hoop niet los Los van wat er komt, komt er redding, want God is met ons.' *When everything falls apart, God's heart still beats. He who conquers, He is with us. So don't lose hope. Whatever may come, there will be rescue, for God is with us.*[22]

These lyrics are hard to translate, because next to this meaning, there is also a literal meaning that can't be translated. In Dutch, the first words literally mean: 'When nothing beats anymore, God's heart beats' and these words affect me deeply. Immediately I see the ultrasound again, where literally nothing was beating anymore, especially no heart. But God is with us. That is exactly the only answer we received in those days and now I am reminded of that again. God is with us. I cry and feel deep gratitude towards this worship band, this atmosphere. I can be here, with all my grief, doubts, anger, unbelief. When I am home a week later and write a blog about this song, I want to show it to the band. I search for them on the internet and find out that the couple who leads the band also lost a child. How awful and also how hopeful for me. They can sing again. I too will be able to sing again.

A little while later we go to another church in our neighbourhood. We turn up tired and feeling a bit cast down. The preacher speaks about what Jesus did for us and ends his sermon by saying we can come to Him, with our sadness as well. It moves me and when the service is over, I speak with the pastor. He says I blamed God and have to confess that. I have to let Amanda go and say thanks to God that she is with Him and doesn't need to make a choice anymore and that she has been spared so much misery. We pray together and I go home with mixed feelings. It is true what he says and necessary to confess my attitude of resistance and anger and blaming, but I also feel the need to hear acknowledgement of how terrible it is.

Yet during the week I observe something has changed in my grief about Amanda. Praying with that preacher, confessing that I blamed God and really thanking God that Amanda is with Him, it did free me somehow. The preacher also said that it isn't good to keep thinking of how it would have been, because it is good as it is now. Amanda is doing well. I still think it is a bit bizarre to think that way, but it does help a bit. I can't help that grief sometimes pops up out of nowhere, but I can consciously choose to not think 'what if'. Amanda is safe. I let her go.

Months later, at a songwriters retreat I talk with a worship leader who also lost a baby. I ask him: 'Sometimes the pain is so overwhelmingly deep that it seems I can't breathe anymore. Do you have that too?' He says: 'Yes, but you have to decide to let go.' He refers to Matthew 11:28-30 and points me to Jesus to find rest for my soul.

Again I feel condemned. Do I really have to just leave it behind, ignore it, and go on? Yet, in the days following I see that when sadness overwhelms me, I indeed have a choice. What do I do when grief comes over me as a wave that is just too high to jump aside for? Do I become passive and allow grief to control me, or do I actively go the Lord, cry, express my grief and surrender it to Him again?

Sometimes I am just not able to do that. Then I don't succeed in letting it go again and hold on to my grief by just doing other things, trying to not think about it, numbing myself. Other times I manage to do it. I picture lifting her little body to heaven again and repeat: 'Lord, I give her to You. She was Yours from the very beginning. I am glad she doesn't have to suffer anymore. I am grateful she is whole with You.'

This is not a once-and-for-all-act, but something I need to do often, again and again. In time passing, we miss her in different ways and our grief and missing her changes and will probably continue to change. Now it is the baby we miss, but then it will be the toddler, the schoolkid, the teenager. Every time I become aware that I miss her, every time this deep pain pops up out of nowhere and takes my breath away, I can decide to let it go again. And when sometimes I am not there yet, I hope I soon will be able to do that again. Because I want to decide to let go.

Take Us with You in Your Unbelief

'Once upon a time there was a pastor from a church somewhere in England.' Hope, our pastor's wife shares a story she heard somewhere. 'One day he wanted to resign. 'Because', he said: 'I don't believe anymore, so I can't go on to be your pastor.' The church council discussed his resignation and came back to him with a response he didn't expect. 'We want you to remain and keep preaching. Just take us into what you think and feel and discover. We will stand around you.' The pastor stayed on and preached about his unbelief and doubt. The congregation indeed continued to stand around him, journeyed with him, listened to him and supported this man. After many months the pastor recovered his faith.'

I listen with tearstained eyes. Hope says she thinks that if the congregation would have responded differently, this pastor would have lost his faith forever. I just had told her that I didn't want to be a worship leader anymore, because I thought I couldn't sincerely lead our congregation in worship now that I am broken, doubtful, angry and unbelieving. But Hope doesn't agree with me. She thinks I should go on. She says I am free to stop, but that I do not have to wait until I have it all together again, until I am full of passion and faith. I can just come with what I have, even when that is not so neat.

I walk home, silent and amazed. I think it really is so mind-blowing and also so reassuring. I still hesitate to lead worship again, but decide to join the team again as a singer, although it feels hypocritical to sing that God is good while my whole being screams: 'Really? Are You good? Why is this happening then?' And although I am afraid the congregation might think that when I am singing along everything is fine again and I want to avoid communicating precisely that.

But isn't church exactly the place where people are allowed to be themselves? Where you can come just as you are, even with all that howls and curses inside of you? In our church they often say: 'First you belong, then you believe, then you behave'. That is the right order: first acceptance, then hopefully faith will follow and from there behaviour can change. And all of that takes a lot of time.

This is how we behave towards seekers, people who don't believe yet. But now I undergo this as a believer, as a leader. I too am allowed to just be there first, with all my pain, grief, brokenness, anger. Even as a leader. Cautiously, guarded, I sing along with the team first. I have my flute there with me, so I can play flute when we are singing songs I cannot sing yet. I seek ways to stay authentic as that is what I chose in the past: I want to be real, I don't want to pretend. So there

I stand. Broken. Afraid of what people might think, because I'm not over it and haven't processed it.

It's going to be a long journey. I take one small step at a time and wrestle with what I bump into. Right now, I lead worship again. There is more room for grief, despair and doubt in the songs I choose, than there was in the past. But I also sing *I raise a hallelujah.* I sing *hallelujah* amidst my doubt, my enemies, my circumstances. Not to pump up myself, not to outvoice myself. But because He is worth it.

Wait Until Comfort Comes

In a newspaper I read: 'Wasn't it C.S. Lewis who wrote that if he needed consolation he could better get a bottle of port?'[23] I immediately underlined it, cut out the article and put it in the folder I have with cut-outs of things I really want to write about some day.

What is comfort really? How do you receive consolation? Since Amanda's death this question keeps coming back. I can't grasp it. I don't find comfort. I barely experience God as comforter and I find, to be honest, also that a bottle of port – wine in my case – gives more comfort. I often crave for wine when the children are in bed and I am alone with my Love, who also doesn't know what to do with his feelings. We often don't find each other and can't comfort each other. We do want to be together and try to seek each other's company. We do that by co-existing with a bottle of wine, by making love or by showing each other articles we find helpful or interesting. Maybe I communicate with my blog in the first place to my Love.

Writing this is quite something. I don't know if I will ever publish this, but if you read it, I apparently did. I must talk about this so you know you are not on your own. Are these not just normal human responses to an incomprehensible reality?

Sometimes I just don't know how to go on anymore. Then grief is so in my face that I can't see anything else. It grabs me by the throat, takes away my breath. I want to run, or to be very angry, or to do addictive things. I don't know what to do with it, so I rather push it away, far away.

It pops up unexpectedly and inconveniently. I walk upstairs, smell something and puff! Suddenly I am a year back in time, I have just given birth and Amanda is still in her cradle in the nursery. Silent. Then I realize: yeah! I have another child! Where is she? At moments like that, it is so very real again that it surprises me. At other moments I enjoy life, and I don't consciously think of her every second of the day either. Still she is always dormant, present. Like a thread that is woven through everything and you can't pull out.

'What if you just let it all be. That you tell God how you feel, how sad you are, how hard it is for you. And that you just sit down and God comes to sit beside you and puts an arm around you.' This is what a dear lady said a few weeks ago when I told her that I didn't know what to do with that deep pain inside of me, whilst I also just want to be there for the children, do my job, live life. Her answer was freeing. It made me think of the song I wrote about earlier: *Just be held.*

If I let it all just be there, I feel the brokenness of my own heart and life. I feel how vulnerable I am and realize I have so many questions. If I let it all just be there, if I become honest and try to welcome God, I realize God indeed stands next to me. He listens. All I have to do is be myself, *with* my pain and my questions, *in* my brokenness and vulnerability.

I don't know what God will do then. That is why I find this so hard. But if I try to 'just let everything be there', I do sense He is here. That He really wants to carry me through this, although it isn't clear to me why things went the way they went and why, even at this moment, so much is going on in our lives.

Some time ago I found a booklet that got my attention because of its Dutch title: *Al treft u 't felst verdriet* (Even though you find the most fierce sorrow). It is originally written in English in 1674 by John Flavel, someone who had to bury many loved ones, including also a child. Out of his faith he tries to encourage: 'Do not rush to shake off the yoke that God has placed on your shoulders. You must not want to be delivered from your grief before God's time. Persevere in patience. When God gives comfort in His time and way, that comfort is often lasting and healing.'[24]

I cry when I read it and see how it's connected to what that lady said to me. I continually try to shake off my grief and to live on as if nothing happened. But it is better to allow the sadness and pain to just be there and welcome God to sit next to me in this. Even though I might not receive answers to my questions. Even though situations don't always change and sickness, death, bullying, divorces and all kinds of other misery keep existing. Because we are broken people. All of whom are allowed to simply be there.

I think that is the comfort. That God is there with us.

Come To the Water

We go to church and sing *Oceans*, a song I used to love:

Spirit lead me where my trust is without borders
Let me walk upon the waters
Wherever You would call me
Take me deeper than my feet can ever wander
And my faith will be made stronger
In the presence of my Saviour

Who does not want to have faith that can move mountains?
Who does not want to have a solid conviction to do God's
will whatever it takes? But now, while we are singing it, I
scream in silence: 'No!' I don't want to anymore. Not if that
means another child dies. Never again.

I am shocked by my reaction. I know God likes to see that
I believe Him, build my life on Him and do whatever He
puts on my heart. I have done quite some things out of a
rock-solid faith. Scary things, things people around me
didn't always agree with, things that cost me, but which I
knew deep down inside that God asked them of me. But

now I do not dare anymore. For the first time I do not manage to get over it myself. I don't want to walk where the water is too deep for my feet to find ground beneath them and where without faith you better stop acting.

The following months I wrestle with this intensely. I keep on singing: 'Still, my soul be still', not because I wholeheartedly believe it, but because it gives words to my desire to trust God. I just cling to the habits I had. I read the Bible and pray every day. I sing the songs I can still sing and go to the meetings and conferences I go to every year, such as the song writers' retreats.

In January 2018, ten months after Amanda's birth, I go to the song writers retreat in Amsterdam. We walk to a prayer room where people pray for the city. I am tired and cast down and super sceptical. I decide that I am not going to pretend, so I will not pray out loud. I am only going to focus my attention on God and I pray silently, from where I am in that moment, not contrived, no 'make-believe', no pretense, no manipulation. If something is really God, then manipulation or exaggeration is unnecessary.

Silently I pray for the city and feel compassion towards addicts, prostitutes, people who don't know God. Then a singer a few seats away from me starts to pray out loud. He prays exactly the same things with the same passion as I was praying for in silence and suddenly I realize that the Holy Spirit is real. That He is really at work here and that it is not for nothing, this praying, this seeking, this trying to submit yourself to God.

The next morning, I join a workshop. The leader invites us to write down everything that is bothering us and then to lay the paper in the middle on the floor to symbolically give all that is worrying us to God. After we have done that, we become quiet and ask God what He wants to show us.

I 'see' a man on the water. I am watching from a distance on the beach myself. It is very calm. There is no strong wind. There are no huge waves. The sun breaks through, right above the man. He stands now in bright sunlight. We tell each other what we saw or thought. Then we pray for more explanation and I am reminded of a song from Live: *Run to the water. I find you there*. That isn't a Christian song. I think it is funny, as this used to be my favourite band in the past and God knows that of course. Only I don't know what to do with it.

We talk with each other and then each go to song writing separately. I don't really know what to do with what I saw, until my buddy says to me: 'Isn't that man Jesus?' I am startled and immediately *Oceans* and my prayers of the past months come to mind. In awe I realize Jesus invites me to walk on the water, in the light.

I wrestle with what this means exactly. I listen to the song *Oceans* again and the last line strikes me: 'in the presence of my Saviour'. That is what my buddy said as well: 'But Ineke, you don't walk alone on that water. God is always there.' It is true. I haven't been left alone. Although what I've been through was terrible, if I look back honestly, I can't recall moments that I was on my own. I always was in the presence of my Saviour.

I kneel down and cry and say that I don't dare, but somewhere deep-down want to, but don't know how. Then I describe what I saw in a song. In the months following I sing it again and again:

Come to the Water
Standing on the beach
I'm almost on my own
Looking at the sea
All is calm and quiet
I see a man out there
Standing on the water
The sun bursts through the sky
He's right there in the spotlight
Saying:

Come to the water
It's where you'll find me
Come to the water
'Cause you'll find me there
Come to the water
Take my hand now
Come to the water
'Cause you'll find me here

I'm still standing there
Looking from afar
Wondering if I should
Accept his invitation
I've been there before
But then the waves were rough
Now it's calm and still
And with some hesitation
I decide to

Come to the water
It's where I'll find him
Come to the water

'Cause I'll find him there
Come to the water
I take his hand now
Come to the water
'Cause I'll find him here

Do I dare to trust again?
To lay my life back in his hands?
As he says 'come to the water
And find me there'
Yes I want to trust again
To lay my life back in his hands.
As he calls me to the water
To walk with him

I come to the water
It's where I find you
Come to the water
'Cause I'll find you there
I come to the water
I take your hand now
Come to the water
'Cause I'll find you here[11]

It helps. I often cry when I sing it, because it sounds desperate rather than full of faith: 'Yes Lord, I want to dare to trust again. Come to me.' But singing and acknowledging this does help.

---

[11] Ineke Marsman-Polhuijs, *Come to the water*

Knowing God Through the Pain

At a gathering I see a clip[12] about God's love for Israel, wherein verses from Isaiah were quoted. While watching and hearing the chorus and the second verse of the song, something happens inside of me.

No I'll never forget you
I'll never forsake you
I will never forget My own
Does a mother forget her baby
Or a woman the child in her womb?
Yet even if she should forget
I will never forget My own

In the clip I see a woman wearing dark clothes, holding a small child in her arms. I feel a deep longing rising up. Suddenly I am straight back in the middle of my mourning. Confused I think: but this song isn't about me! It's about how God longs for His people. I know that very well, but I can't stop crying.

---

[12] Peter en Carin van Essen, *I will never forget you*, www.youtube.com/watch?v=SITAUTC6qTI

When the chorus is repeated, the words resonate inside of me. 'No, I will never forget my own'. And I understand: this *is*, this is *also*, about me. The longing described in this chorus, words exactly how I feel over my stillborn baby.

This song, or I should say: these verses from the Bible, gives me permission to mourn, to feel this deep pain. Of course I know that I don't need permission. But because people sometimes ask, 'if I am over it', I often wonder if I am not too dramatic and if I should feel differently. But the Bible makes it very clear in these verses that it is impossible for a mother to forget her baby and paints a beautiful and accurate picture of what a mother's love is.

And God's love goes deeper than this; much deeper.

God longs more for us than a mother for her child. For a long time I think about how wonderful this is and what it all means. Slowly a shocking truth begins to dawn on me: Knowing what it feels like to lose a child I love so much and longing for a child I will never meet in this life shows me the depth of God's love. It actually gives me more insight into God's love.

Losing Amanda, longing for her, mourning over her, learning to live on without her, trying to find out what I believe and what I hope for and what I live for, leads to me to a deeper understanding of how desperately God desires us to come closer to Him.

Sometime later I discover that I actually have become more convinced that God will never forget me and never leave me. Just as I will never forget my beloved baby girl. So somehow this terrible situation also shows me something of God's love.

God of Hope

As I feel down and tired and unbelieving, I find it hard to write songs. Someone suggests I could ask my pastor what I could write a song about. I decide to do that and James mentions the scripture that is central to our church this year. Romans 15:13. In my Dutch Bible, it says (my translation): 'Now the God of hope may fill you with all joy and peace in believing, so that you will be overflowing in the hope, by the power of the Holy Spirit.' James explains that he has the feeling that the church and actually everybody needs to hear about hope, especially in light of all the news we hear about wars and disasters.

In a sermon he explains that hope in Greek is 'elpidos' and that it means 'expectation of what is certain'. So it doesn't mean hope as in: I hope the weather will be good tomorrow. Because that isn't certain. The hope Romans refers to is certain.

It doesn't speak to me yet. I don't feel hope and I don't have hopeful thoughts and writing a song about hope when you don't feel any hope yourself is quite difficult. I decide to ask the Holy Spirit to guide me because He is the source of hope and strength; that much I understand from this verse.

I immerse myself in the letter to the Romans and read it in all the translations I can find. Because I go to an English-speaking church, I read the text also in different versions in that language. I want to know what it means to expect what is certain. To hope. I read and read and pray that God will show me what it means, and what should be in the song. Because I want to be authentic and don't want to write a song that might be factually true and correct but I can't sing from my heart, I end up in a considerable struggle.

Romans talks about Abraham. He had to wait for years until the promises of God were fulfilled. He kept on hoping. In the text God is called the God of hope Himself. In fact. He *is* hope. He is our hope. It is not necessarily about hoping for our wishes to come true. It's about putting our hopes *on Him*, no matter what will happen.

In my thoughts I hear Cody ask again: 'Do you still trust God?' and I think of what I discovered some time later: What do you trust God for? If you trust Him so that all your plans will succeed, or your wishes come true, or trust your interpretation of what God says is right, there will always come a moment when this trust turns out to be weak. When you trust God Himself, His character, His hand in your life, His promises that He is with you, you have firm ground beneath your feet after all. Whatever happens. Because no one will take you from His hand.

So that's the hope that's certain. He is with me. I put all translations together and chose words, interpret their meaning and write a song that is surprisingly hopeful and yet still acknowledges the despair that still rages in my heart too.

God of Hope
Let the God of hope
Fill us with all joy
Fill us with all peace
As we trust in Him

So that we overflow, overflow in hope
By the power of the Holy Spirit
Fully persuaded that He'll do as He promised
For He Himself is our hope

So that we can rejoice
Can rejoice in trouble
By the power of the Holy Spirit
Fully aware that He's there with us
For He Himself is our hope[13]

In March 2018, a year after Amanda's death, I sing it in church when I lead worship. I become emotional when I sing that last verse: We are fully aware that He's there with us in trouble.

Suddenly I realize that I believe it.

---

[13] Ineke Marsman-Polhuijs, *God of hope*

Processing

How do you process grief? And what does processing mean really? One says that processing the death of a loved one is impossible, someone else gives it a workable meaning. I myself am not sure what to think of it, until I hear Suzan Hilhorst say in an interview on television that after the death of your child you have a big ball of grief in front of you that you cannot take in all at once. You keep taking out one bite at a time and integrate that into your life until that whole ball of sadness has been woven into yourself. In the words of C.S. Lewis: 'I was wrong to say the stump was recovering from the pain of the amputation. I was deceived because it has so many ways to hurt me that I discover them only one by one.'[25]

I keep discovering new things while walking through this land of mourning. At times, grief overwhelms me with the devastating force of a hurricane where I feel completely enveloped and have nowhere to go. At other times it is a nauseous, sneaky, creeping upward feeling where you feel it move from your toes to the corner of your eye into one salty tear that you almost have to squeeze out. I am learning to sit in the pain as if it were contractions. This wave will also pass. The worst thing is that you never know when the next wave will come.

I go to Barbara again. She uses a coaster as an image for grief. She holds it right in front of her eyes and shows that when you do that, you don't see anything else and that is good. It's good to look at your grief. Then she stretches out her arm, still holding the coaster, and says, 'After a while you can keep it a little further away from you and see other things around you.' Then she places the coaster next to her on the table for a moment and says: 'There will come a time when there will be moments when you can put it away or carry it with you in a special place. You still have it, but it is not visible.'

She encourages me to do something with my grief. How is me being the mother of Amanda woven into my life? Maybe I can creatively give form to that or symbolically do something with that in nature. I could also really ask the questions I have and thoroughly study them. Eventually I will be able to look at what good comes out of it. Amanda's death wasn't good, but God can do something good with it.

I go home, pleased with what Barbara told me. At this moment, grief is still very much 'in my face'. I can't see much else. But it helps to know that in the long run I can keep it further from me or carry it with me invisibly. I do write a lot already, so I think that if I want to work on this creatively, I can best do that by writing. I blog and discover it helps to give words to what I go through and allow

152

others to read it. By how people respond, I find out I give others words for their grief as well.

Processing is working and it doesn't mean forgetting, dismissing or ignoring. I am still the mother of Amanda and denying that would be ridiculous. Manu Keirse, who wrote many beautiful books about grief and gives very good talks, started to use another word for processing that is hard to translate in English. It is a word ('overleven' literally: *surviving*) that doesn't have the connotation to 'get over it' but is more about living on, surviving the loss.

Maybe it is just a matter of speaking, of definition. What matters is, that you learn to live with your sadness. As Marijke Serné puts it: 'I think mourning is a way to deal with your grief. A way that suits you.'[26] In June 2019 I came to this conclusion:

> Perhaps mourning is the journey you take to get your mind and feelings back in line together. Perhaps mourning in faith is the journey you take to get your mind and feelings back in line together with God. I hope I have been mourning in faith, that I am mourning with faith. That I mourned without excluding God but involving Him in everything. Honest, straightforward, sincere. And allowing Him to work in this. In the mess. In the misery, the sorrow, the pain.

Amanda Day

'Grief is a normal and healthy way to answer loss. It makes you feel how connected you are and that this bond cannot be broken without pain.'

(Riet Fiddelaers-Jasper)[27]

I think it is important not to ignore your grief, but to face it. And if you can do something with it, you are processing. You give meaning to it. A mourning father said it like this:

> 'Mourning is taking the pain instead of running from the pain. Making contact with the loss and on a deep level feeling how much it hurts. You really have to touch it within yourself. You need others to be able to do this, you can't do this alone. It needs an encounter with other people. You need to really want this yourself as well. Somewhere you must be aware that you want to face your loss.'[28]

I regularly take time to do things one-on-one with my children. From now on, I decide to also take 'mamma-

Amanda-time'. I cannot address every wave of grief, because my life rumbles on with the living children in my home. But on Thursday my kids have lunch at school.[14] Then I can allow grief to come to the surface and face it.

So now Thursday is Amanda day. I bike to the grave or do something else that helps me to live with this sadness. For instance, I decide to make a photo album, the way I did for my living children as well. I start with a photo of the imprint of her feet. In November 2017 I write this poem underneath:

Although your feet never walked
not even moved
when you came
Still you crawled into our world
moved us
set us aflame

You left an imprint
a trace that is ingrained
I can talk about it for hours
so big is our happiness and loss
Our happiness, because you were welcome, perfect and beautiful
So many times we have been thankful for you, you were a gift
And our loss, because we would have loved to see you grow up here
See you play and joke around with the other children
Entrusting you to the earth from which God formed you was the hardest thing there is
But no matter how small you were, your fragile existence

---

[14] At many primary schools in Holland, kids go home for lunch on schooldays.

also was your powerful testimony
You proved the existence of a Creator
You were formed so wonderfully in my womb
You proved the existence of Love
So deep is our pride and our grief since you died

Although your feet never walked
not even moved
when you came
Still you left an imprint
A trace
And my heart testifies of it

Keeping Silent

'Sadness that is no longer touched is believed to pass more quickly. However, this attitude misunderstands that grief usually will only be processed by expressing it.'

(Manu Keirse)[29]

'How old are your children?' A kind woman asks me at a birthday party. I hesitate but decide to tell their ages closing with: 'and the youngest has passed away.' A moment of silence. Then she asks: 'Oh, what age would that one be now?' Relieved and grateful I tell her, and she answers: 'Gosh, how terrible' and I say: 'Yes, indeed'. It is quiet again. We both don't know what else to say and go on to talk about other things.

Sometimes people respond so well to what is so bad. Sometimes the sadness and your child are allowed to just be there and you can talk about it if you want to. Because it is what it is. Not naming her does not take away the reality of her absence. The grief, her place in our family, that we would have brought another child with us if she had stayed alive, all that is just there. If others don't acknowledge that or keep it silent (I don't know what to say myself either), they ignore an essential part of who we are now.

'The elephant is always there, until we recognize him. By ignoring him, those who grieve isolate themselves and the ones who could offer comfort, creating distance instead. Both sides need to open up. Speaking with sincerity and empathy is a good start.'[30] I find it makes a huge difference whether Amanda is mentioned or not. If she is mentioned, if she is recognized as belonging to us, we can be somewhat relaxed. Then we can laugh and enjoy too, because we can cry also. Unfortunately, the opposite is also true. If I have the feeling that I am not allowed to mention her and cannot cry if I have to, I almost can't laugh as well. I have to suppress all my feelings, so sometimes at parties or meetings, I sit on the sidelines, a bit indifferent and disconnected to what is going on, if I can get myself to come in the first place.

Someone told us we shouldn't share that we lost a child, because that makes others feel so uncomfortable. I nodded understandingly. I often try to consider everyone's feelings and I thought: yes, I should probably do that. But it keeps bugging me. Wait a minute, it makes others feel uncomfortable? For how long then, a few minutes, maybe a day? Is that really that bad? It *is* very uncomfortable, isn't it? That other person only suffers from that for a short time. We have to live with it every day.

When I keep silent about Amanda, I do more than shielding someone else. I ignore that I am the mother of five children and that I often think of Amanda and miss her. It feels like betrayal of her, my Love, and my other children. They have another sister. He has three daughters. We are so proud of her. So happy that she has been here. We need that to be acknowledged. Besides that, it is especially on celebrations that the missing pops up and with that also the need to be allowed space for that. 'The deceased is present, precisely there, where his or her absence is felt most heavily.'[31] That is why parties are so hard. Especially when we celebrate life, religious feasts, birthdays, anniversaries, weddings; if we want to celebrate happily, the grief for Amanda arises. She is painfully present in her absence.

Besides this, I think it is important to not keep silent about Amanda because there are many babies who die around birth. There is a lot of silent grief about silent babies. When I talk about my little girl, I often hear stories about other women who have lost a child. There are many older people who silently mourn their dead children. By keeping silent, their grief didn't become less. When I talk about my little girl, others have room to share about who they've lost.

When I cycle to the hairdresser one day and think of how I will respond if she asks me how many children I have, I decide to say 'five' and if she asks more questions, I will tell her about Amanda. I don't know what is going on in her life, but if I can talk openly about sad things, I give her space to do the same if she wants to. It helps to make up my mind about this upfront, even though a little bit later it turns out she doesn't want to talk at all.

Months later I notice I've lost some of my ability to tolerate and adjust to other people. I find it harder and harder to accept the silence of others. I begin to avoid people who pretend Amanda never existed. I always wanted to be there for others, however they treated me and by God's grace I often managed to do that. But now I cannot anymore. If I have to keep silent about her, when she is so real to me, why should I listen to their story?

Again I need grace. More grace, more understanding, more space in my heart. Because I still believe we have to treat others as we want to be treated ourselves and not as we are treated ourselves. That is a huge difference, I now find out again. And you can never know *why* people act the way they do. Often there are good intentions, even though good intentions can really hurt as well.

So I bow my head again, pour out my sadness and anger with God who knows it already, to receive more grace and more love to again be there for the other, however he or she is behaving towards me. Again I wonder about the thin line between grief and self-pity. Or should you perhaps go through self-pity first before you can reach the grief? Keeping quiet is pointless, I know for sure, because that suffocates even more. So here I am again, broken but real, prepared to make the effort to treat and speak with others with grace. Even when they keep silent about my beloved child.

Comparing

Sometimes I tend to minimize my own grief because others went through worse things than I did. It reminds me of what other kids used to ask me when I was young, because I am hearing impaired: 'would you rather be deaf or blind?' I stammered that being blind probably was worse, used as I was to my bad ears. Still, hearing impairment is a tough handicap, I can tell you. And I think a blind person would love to see and also wouldn't want to be deaf.

Sometimes someone tells me it's good Amanda died so soon and I didn't have the chance to get to know her and get attached. Sometimes one of my children cries because classmates say it isn't that bad their sister died, as she wasn't even born yet. It hurts. To us the sister is Amanda, and the grief to not know her and to not know how she would have been now, that's just grief.

Sometimes I wrestle with ugly jealousy when another bereaved mother tells her child lived for a couple of hours, or weeks or even years. But her grief of course isn't less because she has memories she can cherish and she had a place to go to with her love. Just as my grief isn't less because I missed having that. Grief is just grief.

Comparing destroys. It isolates. When my grief can be there and the grief of someone else can be there too, then connection can happen. If shared sorrow is half a sorrow, then unshared sorrow is maybe double sorrow. I make up my mind to acknowledge grief for what it is, without comparison or judgement. I even think that can be healing. Because when grief can be there and is acknowledged, then this gives room for other feelings such as compassion. I discover that in a peculiar way.

The mother of a classmate of one of my children died after a bedridden sickness. There will be a spiritual counsellor in their Roman Catholic school to talk with the children. She will also be available for the parents. My children are annoyed about it. There wasn't something like this when Amanda died. I share honestly that I thought the same. But I am also ashamed that I thought that. I think I will join the children at school and will decide there and then if I will go to this meeting.

When I enter the classroom of my child, I see the grief of others and suddenly feel the grief about Amanda grabbing my throat. I feel a strong need for attention and am very ashamed about that. A mother died now. This isn't about Amanda. I go to the counsellor. There is only one other mother so I dare to tell honestly what I think and feel. Full of understanding she says: 'When someone dies, it touches the grief that already was there. It is very normal that the grief about Amanda suddenly pops up heavily in you and the children.' She advises me to look at the album of Amanda tonight, together with the children, and to remember Amanda together. 'Because', she says 'Only if you give room to your own sadness, can you sympathize with others.'

That night we look into the booklets the classmates made for my children when Amanda had died and we look in Amanda's photo album. It's good for us indeed. We cry about Amanda and then we pray for the girl who has to live on without her mother.

You cannot cross out one sadness against the other. It takes me a lot of time and attention to accept that my grief is my grief and should just be there, no matter what others think. I cannot stop being the mother of my child, even if she is deceased and even though she did not even live outside of my womb. As another parent puts it: 'How can I miss someone who was never here? How can someone who was never here still be here? You never walked around here, you didn't crow, you didn't take any steps, you didn't fall here. And yet: you were here, you belong here.'[32]

I have a need for acknowledgment and confirmation. But whether others think my grief can be here or not, it doesn't diminish the fact that the grief just exists. Especially in my relationship with God I find out it is important to just acknowledge those feelings and to cry the tears that are still there, even though it feels sometimes as if it is an unending stream.

My Love sends me an email from the city council, with this remark: 'With a smile and a tear. She's there.' Amanda is registered in the BRP, the basic registration of persons of our city. She is acknowledged as an existing person. She is just as much gone as before but still she is our child. She is a daughter and a sister and now she is listed by the government as officially part of our family. It does our hearts so much good. She belongs to us, she is a part of me. What a wonderful and sad feeling that gives. With a smile and a tear. She's there.

Memories

I'm in the car, on my way to the music shop. I usually don't enjoy driving that much, but today I do. I finally do what I have postponed, the weather is good and the road is not too busy. A moment of clearing the head and I really need that right now.

Suddenly I smell something and I'm triggered. I am back in time. Amanda. I smell a scent that is connected to her and suddenly I can't think of anyone else. I see myself in her room again, sitting at the cradle, wondering, feeling love, expressing sorrow. I take her in my hands and dedicate her again to Him who gave her, her short life.

I am quite shocked and want to sob like a small child. Self-pity and determination compete for precedence. It would be good to cry again, I think. But it is not convenient right now. I am on my way to a music store full of tough, creative men among whom I often feel like an amateurish fool. Having a tearful face and red eyes will not help.

This again is a wave just like the books about mourning mention often. A wave of grief forcibly and unexpectedly rolls over you and makes you lose your balance and orientation completely. But it is not only awkward and sad. I feel joy as well. This scent makes me happy, because she made me happy and in this scent for a brief moment she is very near.

The memory of me holding her in my hands also pops up at other times. I see myself sitting in her room, next to her cradle. I look at her and take her in my hands, even though it is pointless as she is not aware. I look at her, attentively and I'm amazed. That she is so tiny, but so complete and has everything a human being normally has. I thank God He didn't do an unfinished job but made the effort to make her this beautiful.

I see myself sitting. This image sticks with me. I want to do justice to God who made her this beautiful and to the pain that is there and testifies of love that doesn't stop in death. Even though I know she is safe and cherished and I wouldn't want it any other way for her anymore, the hole in my heart is still there. And also the love that was born together with her.

I want to make a song about this. For a very long time I can't find the rest to do it, but when I am alone in my sister's house during a school holiday to work at this book, I decide to use that time first to finish this song.

Only I cried
I held her tiny body in my hand
Admired her with awe and love
Amazed by how she looked and lay asleep
Reflecting life while she was gone

Only I moved Only I cried
Only I was watching her

She did not look
Made no sound at all
She could not receive my care

I held her tiny body in my hand
Hoping her heart would beat again
But she just lay there still and beautiful
Declaring wonders to my woe
Only I moved Only I cried
Only I felt crushed inside
She did not feel
Wasn't there at all
Still she showed me there's a God

She was wonderfully made
She was crafted by an artist
A masterpiece of God

She called to worship Him
In all my ache and grief
She testified of God

Only I move
Only I cry
Only I can feel the void
She has no need
She is safe with Him
She just taught me He is God

I hold her tiny imprint in my heart
And honour Him who knows my pain[15]

---

[15] Ineke Marsman-Polhuijs, *Only I cried*

Nothing Is Wasted

'Sometimes your sadness is so big, you can't feel anything else', a friend said to me when I told her that I couldn't find God anymore. Someone else encouraged me to walk through the valley. Don't run, don't sit down, just keep on walking. It helped me to face what I came across on my way and in my emotions and unexpected thoughts.

It is true you need to search for God and that you have to try to welcome Him. But how grateful I am that He doesn't let us go and that He comes to us. We should not drag ourselves out of the valley but encourage each other to keep on walking through this deep valley of darkness.

Jerry Sittser wrote: 'I have grieved long and hard and intensely. But I have found comfort knowing that the sovereign God, who is in control of everything, is the same God who has experienced the pain I live with every day. No matter how deep I sink, I will always find God there. He is not far above my suffering, but He comes to me when I'm in difficulty.'[33]

It took a long time, but now I can say this after him. I felt I had lost everything and had to reinvent everything. I wondered if I still believed and how to go on. Now I can say that He did not leave me alone and that it is true that I was never, ever alone. I have changed, I had to get to know myself again. But God was always there with me.

'However many layers have been peeled off and however wrestled through it is at this moment, in an important sense, my faith became my basis after all. It doesn't mean that with that I suddenly have answers. But for those who believe, the questions might not have an answer, but they do have an address. I am convinced that I can ask them to someone who one day will answer. I choose to believe that, just as I choose to believe that I will see my mother again one day. This does not annul anything. It doesn't diminish the sadness. Here on earth I will not see her back. What is taken from me, continues to be taken. But it is not a black hole without an end. Until that time the pain, the misunderstanding, the sadness and the despair will stay. I have to deal with that. Because I do have to live in the here and now.'[34]

Looking back now, I see that God carried us when we received the news, at birth, in the days thereafter. I begged God for what we sang at the funeral: 'Carry me through the deep water, where I can't stand anymore.'[16] I didn't feel it. For a long time, I did not experience God at all and

---

[16] This is a Dutch song. Original lyrics are: 'Draag mij door het diepe water, waar ik zelf niet meer kan staan.'
https://www.youtube.com/watch?v=83SFLi3uljk

everything I believed and thought was unsettled. I had to work, looking for what could still be useful from what used to be so obvious, and it took time. A lot of time. I felt alone. Sometimes also deserted. But somehow now I am convinced that although my life has changed and Amanda has a place in my heart that I cannot give to anyone else, He guides me and never leaves me alone.

I learned to say: I am still God's child. I don't live out of what I feel, but out of what I believe. I should not look inwardly, but up. And when I look back, I see that God continually gave me something in the words of people. It helps to talk, to cautiously do things and trying to involve God in that. It is important to be honest and to complain and to cry and to allow God, even though I do not always know how to do that.

In my book I quote a song I wrote myself and could not sing anymore after Amanda's death. Nowadays I can sing it again and it has a new dimension now. Amanda brought a lot of grief and pain into our lives. But also a lot of joy and depth. We wouldn't want her to not have been here and her death eventually enlarged our heart indeed, as Jerry Sittser writes: 'I did not get over the loss of my loved ones; rather, I absorbed the loss into my life, like soil receives decaying matter, until it became a part of who I am. Sorrow took up permanent residence in my soul and enlarged it.'[35]

I can sing this song again now and want to encourage you with it. Remember God is with you, even when you're not feeling it.

Nothing is Wasted with God
Nothing is wasted with God
Nothing is wasted by God
Thank You, Lord
You keep us in peace
In perfect peace

Nothing is wasted with God
Nothing is wasted by God
Thank You, Lord
That even in times
We thought we were lost You were there

Your word is true
Your love is real
You turn ashes to beauty
Nakedness you cover
Shame You take away
Thank you, Lord[17]

---

[17] Ineke Marsman-Polhuijs, *Nothing is wasted with God*

Recommendations

How can you help people who suffer a great loss? A lot of books have been written about this and in my list of literature you find some I would recommend. My book was mainly about how I tried to keep on believing during the whole process. But a few things that helped us, I list below.

- ❖ Say that it is horrible. 'Sometimes the best thing for a grieving heart is for someone to say 'Yeah' and validate how hard it all is. We don't need to be fixed; we just need to be accepted in our brokenness.'[36]
- ❖ Don't say: 'You need to seek help' too soon. Ask questions first: 'How are you today?' (not: 'How are you', that is too big and complicated to answer), or: 'Would you like to talk about him or her now?'
- ❖ People who are grieving need loving company. 'No one expects you to take away the pain. The only choice you have is if you let the grieving person deal with his pain and sorrow alone or with your support and understanding.'[37]

❖ Yes, we do have to seek God and try to welcome Him in our lives. But He doesn't let us go. Trust in that. Don't push or drag someone out or through the valley. Accept that one needs to walk through it. Don't force someone to run through it, and check now and then that he or she hasn't sat down. Encourage them to keep on walking through this deep dark valley of darkness and keep believing that God sees you and me and them and holds us.

❖ Do not compare. It isolates. If your grief can be there, and the grief of the other person too, then connection can grow.

❖ Don't judge. You have no idea how you would respond if you went through what the other person goes through. So try to empathize, have sympathy, and ask questions.

❖ Acknowledge the situation. Do not diminish or exaggerate. It is allowed to be there. The grief and also the uncomfortable feelings it might give you. It is okay.

❖ Don't be too scared to make mistakes. Just love. True love casts out fear. Don't let fear guide you, but love.

❖ Because grief can pop up unexpectedly, people's self-confidence is subverted. It helps if a person knows they can allow their sorrow to exist and express it at those times.

❖ Anger, irritability, exhaustion are very normal when people are grieving. Manu Keirse writes: 'If people can make clear that these feelings are normal for those who suffer great loss, then he or she has space to step by step climb out of the valley. The mourning person needs to feel that he is allowed to slow down physically, emotionally and also socially.'[38]

LITERATURE

I could give a long list of books and in the footnotes you will already find a lot. I didn't keep track of all the books I was reading from the beginning and also I do not find every book recommendable. So I just give a few suggestions:

∞ Kathy Beckers Mansell, *Rouwen na het verlies van je baby*, Heeze, 2017. Kathy Beckers-Mansell lost her first child herself and became a grief therapist. She wrote two books about loss. Together with Jacques van Herten she also made a beautiful documentary that is well worth watching. You can find them here:
https://steunpuntnova.nl/zorgverleners/videos/

∞ Adriel Booker, *Grace like Scarlett; Grieving with Hope after Miscarriage and Loss*, Michigan, 2018. An honest book about miscarriages and stillborn babies, about suffering and grief.

∞ Victor E. Frankl, *Man's Search for Meaning*. (First printed in German, 1946). A book that gives hope and insights in how people think and what thoughts are helpful and what thoughts are not.

∞ Christine Geerinck-Verkammen, *Stille baby's. Rouwverwerking bij doodgeboorte en zwangerschapsafbreking,* Amsterdam, 2000, 2001. A very clear book with a lot of information for parents who lost a child as well as those around them.

∞ Manu Keirse, *Helpen bij verlies en verdriet; een gids voor het gezin en de hulpverlener,* Tielt, 2017. I read a lot of Manu Keirse and his insights and suggestions are a must for everyone if you ask me. In this book you find summarized a lot of what he has said.

∞ C.S. Lewis, *A Grief Observed,* 1961. Not a hopeful book, but an honest report of how a grieving, believing man mourns for his wife.

∞ Dawn Siegrist Waltman, *In a Heartbeat.* A book with small chapters you can read at your own pace. Sometimes a bit simplistic, but worth reading still.

∞ Jerry Sittser, *A Grace Disguised.* 1995. A very honest book with a lot of great insights about mourning and faith.

∞ Judith Stoker, *Doorleven; omgaan met verlies en rouw,* Aalten, 2019. This book I read after writing my book, but is very accessible, written with compassion from a Christian point of view for people who have to deal with loss and those who want to help them.

∞ Philip Yancey, *The question that never goes away; What is God up to in a world of such tragedy and pain?* Grand Rapids, 2013. Very honest and well thought through. It deals with deep questions as to why and suffering. Well worth reading.

Footnotes

Sometimes I found the quotes of the original English text on the internet. As for the other quotes of books I read in Dutch, the translations are mine.

———————————

[1] C.S. Lewis, *Verdriet, dood en geloof,* Franeker, 1989, p. 57 (Original title: *A grief observed*), translation found on the internet

[2] Proverbs 24:16 NKJV

[3] Kathy Beckers-Mansell, *Rouwen na het verlies van je baby; blijvend verlangen naar je kind van de toekomst,* Heeze, 2017, p. 146

[4] Ezekiel 24:15vv

[5] Psalms 139:16 NIV

[6] Royal Singers, *We are not alone.* www.youtube.com/watch?v=oPdtda-ZhZw

[7] Max Lucado, *Webster, de bange spin.* Barneveld, 2006 (In English: Webster, the scaredy spider).

[8] https://www.youtube.com/watch?v=WYoYJsAVixE

[9] Jerry Sittser, *Verborgen genade; hoe de ziel kan groeien door verlies,* Hoenderloo, 2005, p. 105. (Original title: *A grace disguised*)

[10] Jeanette Rietberg i.s.m. *Maria Pel, Altijd een kind tekort; handboek bij zwangerschap na babysterfte,* Breukelen, 2014

[11] A.F.Th. van der Heijden, *Tonio. Een requiemroman,* Amsterdam, p. 389

[12] Max Lucado, *Vertrouw maar op mij,* Kampen, p. 39 (Original title: *You'll get this*)

[13] I sang this song in Dutch and this line is in the lyrics of the Dutch version of this song.

[14] Manu Keirse, *Vingerafdruk van verdriet,* Tielt, 2012, p. 36

[15] Jerry Sittser, Verborgen genade; hoe de ziel kan groeien door verlies, Hoenderloo, 2005, p. 18 (Original title: A grace disguised)

[16] C.S. Lewis, *Verdriet, dood en geloof,* Franeker, 1989, p. 9, Translation found on the internet (Original title: *a Grief observed*)

[17] Suzan Hilhorst, *Sara en Liv,* Amsterdam, 2017, p. 143-144

[18] Hebrews 12:1

[19] EMDR means Movement Desensitization and Reprocessing. It is a treatment wherin you share your memory of a trauma while being distracted at the same time. Then there is a small break to see what comes to mind. When that happens, you work with what came up.

The aim of the distraction while sharing is to make your feelings less fierce while reminded of them.

[20] https://discoveryseries.org/courses/why-christians-doubt/ p. 21-22

[21] Ann Voskamp, *Gebroken leven*, Franeker, 2016, p. 52

[22] Lev, *God is met ons*, Music & Lyrics: Mattijn Buwalda, 2015, https://youtu.be/k0XC6r6Xieg

[23] Gert van de Wege in, *Gulliver; bijlage van het Nederlands Dagblad*, Friday January 26, 2018, p.10

[24] John Flavel, *Al treft u 't felst verdriet; troost in dagen van rouw*, Apeldoorn, 2017 p. 9 (Original title: *A Token for Mourners*)

[25] C.S. Lewis, *Verdriet, dood en geloof*, Franeker, 1989, p. 59, translation found on the internet (Original title: A Token for Mourners,).

[26] Marijke Serné, *Ondersteboven & binnenstebuiten*, Utrecht, 2017, p. 25

[27] Riet Fiddelaers-Jasper, *Met mijn ziel onder de arm; tussen welkom heten en afscheid nemen*, Heeze, p. 10

[28] Freek in: Kathy Beckers-Mansell, *Kind van de toekomst; verhalen over de impact van het verlies van een baby*, Velp, 2013, p. 145

[29] Manu Keirse, *Vingerafdruk van verdriet*, Tielt, 2012, p.19

[30] Shery Sandberg m.m.v. Adam Grant, *Optie B*, Amsterdam, 2017, p. 54

[31] Marinus van den Berg, *Rouwen in de tijd*, Utrecht, 2012. p. 28

[32] Casper van Koppenhagen, *Ik had je gedacht mijn kind*, Amersfoort, p. 17-18

[33] Jerry Sittser, *Verborgen genade; hoe de ziel kan groeien door verlies*, Hoenderloo, 2005, p. 165, translation partially found on the internet, partially mine (Original title: *A grace disguised*)

[34] In: Coen Verbraak, *De achterblijvers*, De bezige bij, p. 187

[35] Jerry Sittser, *Verborgen genade; hoe de ziel kan groeien door verlies*, Hoenderloo, 2005, p. 38-39, translation found on the internet

[36] Adriel Booker, *Grace like Scarlett*, Grand Rapids, p. 71

[37] Manu Keirse, *Helpen bij verlies en verdriet*, Tielt, p. 37

[38] Manu Keirse, *Vingerafdruk van verdriet*, Tielt, 2012, p. 55